Transparency Masters and Exercises
for
Baron and Byrne

Social Psychology
Understanding Human Interaction

Seventh Edition

Prepared by
Bem P. Allen
Western Illinois University

Gene F. Smith
Western Illinois University

Allyn and Bacon

Boston • London • Toronto • Sydney • Tokyo • Singapore

Table of Contents

Preface

<u>Transparency Masters</u>

Exercise Handouts

Chapter One

Ex. 2   Common Sense Notions
Ex. 3   Wilson and Donnerstein Experimental Descriptions
Ex. 5   Scenarios for Identifying Independent and Dependent Variables
Ex. 5A   Critical Thinking Questions

Chapter Two

Ex. 1   A Story From Long Ago
Ex. 2   Demonstrating Actor/Observer Differences
Ex. 4   Exam Rating Scale
Ex. 6   Applying Attribution to Everyday Situations

Chapter Three

Ex. 3   Demonstration of Self-Reference Effect

Chapter Four

Ex. 1   Trustworthiness of Occupations
Ex. 5   Self-Monitoring Scale (See Ex. 1 in Chapter 5)

Chapter Five

Ex. 1   Self-Monitoring Scale
Ex. 3   Log Sheet for Self-Description

Chapter Six

Ex. 1   Is There Racism At This School?
Ex. 2A   Gender Scale
Ex. 2B   Race Scale

Chapter Seven

Ex. 2   Interpersonal Orientation Scale
Ex. 3   Romanticism Scale
Ex. 4   Similarity/Attraction Scale
Ex. 5   Simpson's Dating Survey

Preface

The two sets of items contained herein can be of great use to instructors adopting Baron and Byrne, *Social Psychology: Understanding Human Interaction, Seventh Edition.* First, the transparency masters listed in the Instructor's Section of the Annotated Instructor's Edition (AIE) of *Social Psychology* are included. Each transparency is either a table or figure from the text, or a figure made especially to complement the text. These transparencies will provide the instructor with a useful supplement for lectures, and also aid students in understanding the material.

Also included is a set of materials relating to the exercises in the Instructor's Section of the AIE of *Social Psychology*. All the information needed to use them is contained in the "Classroom Exercises" section for each chapter. These handouts are ready to duplicate and represent all the materials students will need to participate in the exercises.

Correlation versus Causation

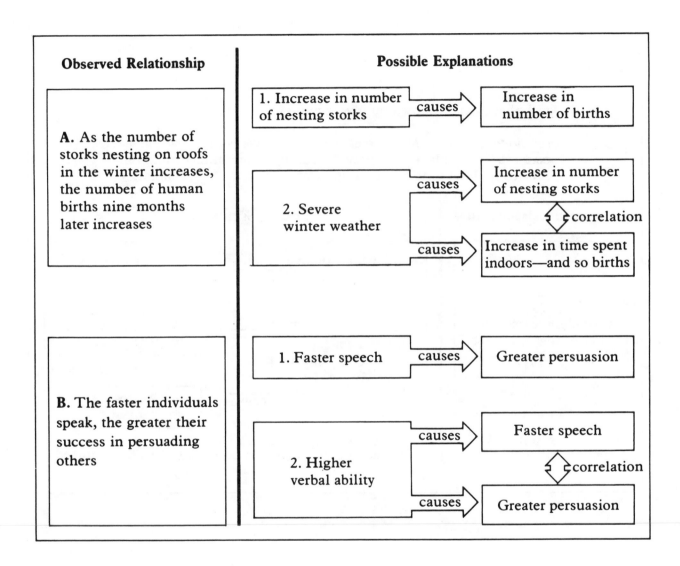

Observed Relationship

Possible Explanations

A. As the number of storks nesting on roofs in the winter increases, the number of human births nine months later increases

1. Increase in number of nesting storks →causes→ Increase in number of births

2. Severe winter weather →causes→ Increase in number of nesting storks ◇correlation →causes→ Increase in time spent indoors—and so births

B. The faster individuals speak, the greater their success in persuading others

1. Faster speech →causes→ Greater persuasion

2. Higher verbal ability →causes→ Faster speech ◇correlation →causes→ Greater persuasion

Hypothesis: Exposure to violent television programs causes an increase in level of aggression shown by young viewers.

Correlational Strategy: Measure aggressiveness, via peer ratings. Measure exposure to T.V. violence, via parental ratings. Compute correlation coefficient to determine relationship between above two variables.

Observed Relationship	Possible Explanations

As the number of violent T.V. programs viewed increases, the level of aggressiveness displayed increases

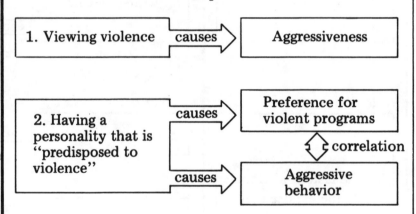

1. Viewing violence — causes → Aggressiveness

2. Having a personality that is "predisposed to violence" — causes → Preference for violent programs ⇕ correlation — causes → Aggressive behavior

∴ No causal conclusion can be unequivocally supported.

Hypothesis: Exposure to violent television programs causes an increase in level of aggression shown by young viewers.

Experimental Strategy:

I. Manipulate violence content of T.V. viewing.

    A. Randomly assign one group to view program with much violent content.

    B. Randomly assign second group to view program with little (or no) violent content.

II. Measure aggressiveness via appropriate test.

III. Test for difference between the two groups.

Observed Relationship

Only Possible Explanation

Children who viewed the violent T.V. programs were more aggressive than those who viewed the nonviolent program

Viewing violence → causes → Aggressiveness

∴ A causal conclusion is supported

Confounding of Variables: A Dangerous Trap for Unwary Experimenters

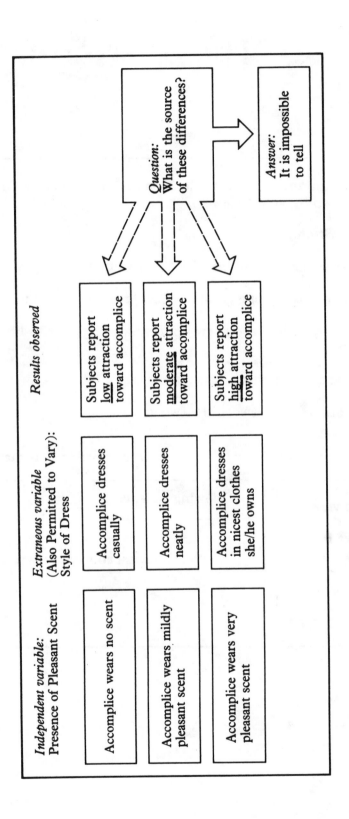

Correlation versus Causation: A Subtle but Crucial Distinction

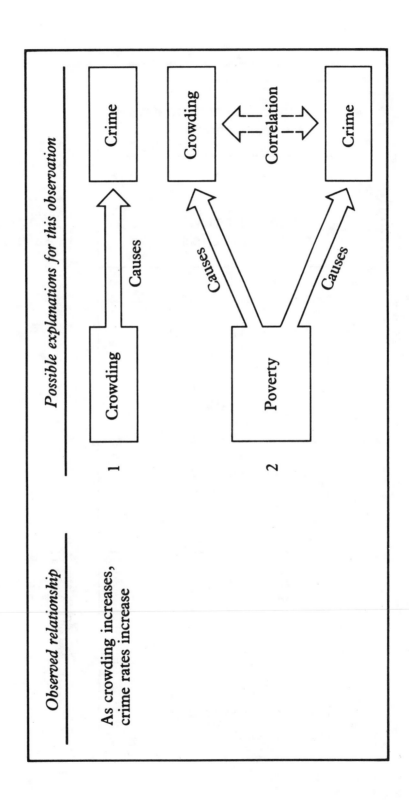

Observed relationship

As crowding increases, crime rates increase

Possible explanations for this observation

1 Crowding → Causes → Crime

2 Poverty → Causes → Crowding
   Poverty → Causes → Crime
   Crowding ←- Correlation -→ Crime

Correspondent Inference: When Do We Infer the Traits of Others?

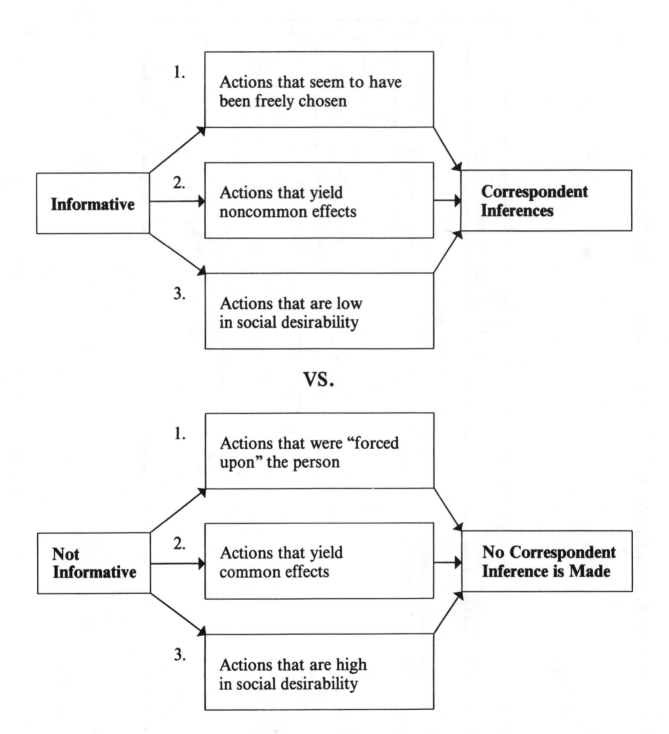

Informative

1. Actions that seem to have been freely chosen

2. Actions that yield noncommon effects

3. Actions that are low in social desirability

Correspondent Inferences

VS.

Not Informative

1. Actions that were "forced upon" the person

2. Actions that yield common effects

3. Actions that are high in social desirability

No Correspondent Inference is Made

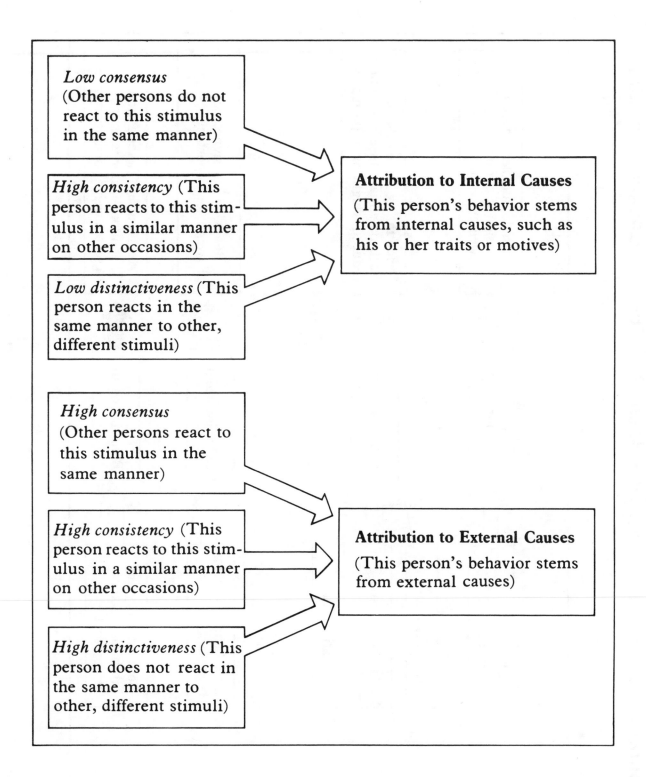

Discounting and Augmenting: Two Basic Principles of Causal Attribution

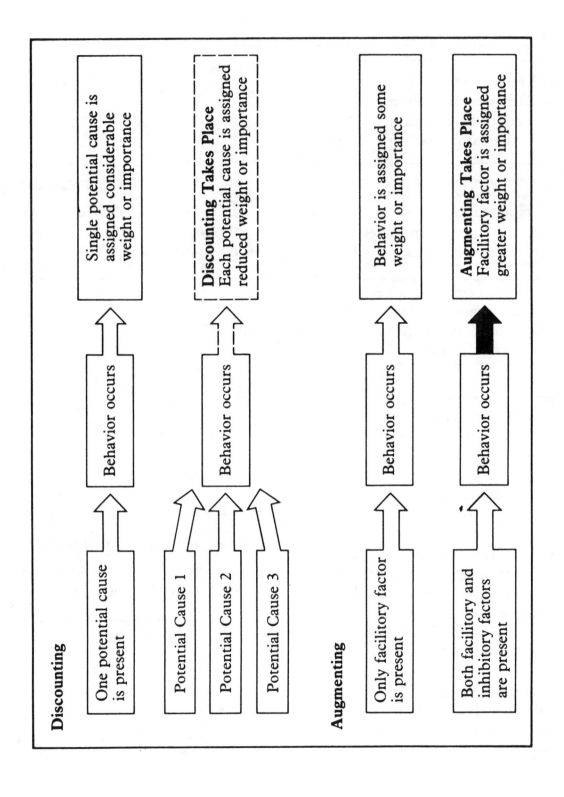

1. **Behavior that is observed:
   Sue is arguing with Professor James**

2. **Consensus, consistency, and
   distinctiveness information:**

   A. Almost no one argues with Professor James.

   B. Sue argues with Professor James on other occasions

   C. Sue also argues with other professors.

3. **Which statement below best explains
   Sue's arguing with Professor James?**

   A. Something about Sue is the cause.

   B. Something about Professor James is the cause

1. **Behavior that is observed:
   Lori is arguing with Professor Ward**

2. **Consensus, consistency, and
   distinctiveness information**

   A. Many people argue with Professor Ward.

   B. Lori argues with Professor Ward on other occasions.

   C. Lori does not argue with other professors.

3. **Which statement below best explains
   Lori's arguing with Professor Ward?**

   A. Something about Lori is the cause.

   B. Something about Professor Ward is the cause

1. Behavior that is observed: Ann is arguing with Professor Sanders

2. Consensus, consistency, and distinctiveness information:

A. Almost no one argues with Professor Sanders.

B. Ann argues with Professor Sanders on other occasions.

C. Ann does not argue with other professors.

3. Which statement below best explains Ann's arguing with Professor Sanders?

A. Something about Ann is the cause.

B. Something about Professor Sanders is the cause.

(No simple attribution seems logical; instead, we may require some type of person/situation interaction explanation.)

Self-Schemata and Memory

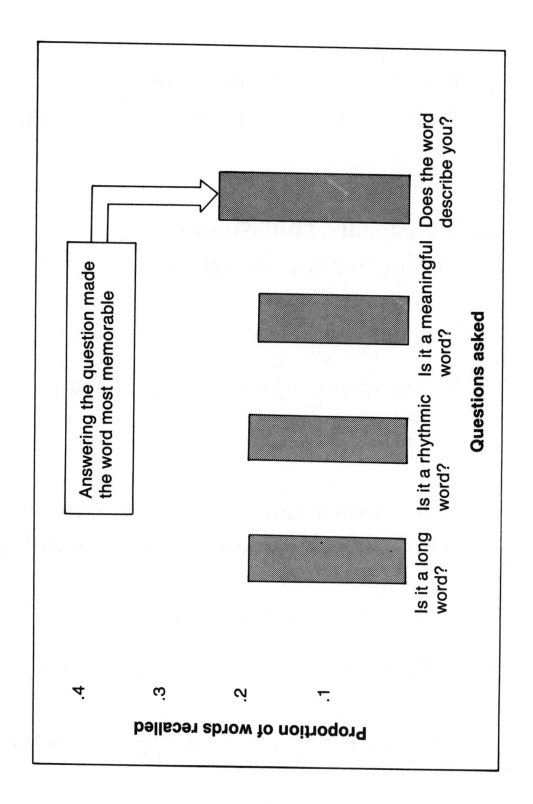

Proportion of words recalled

Answering the question made the word most memorable

| Is it a long word? | Is it a rhythmic word? | Is it a meaningful word? | Does the word describe you? |

Questions asked

Mental Simulations and Sympathy for Victims

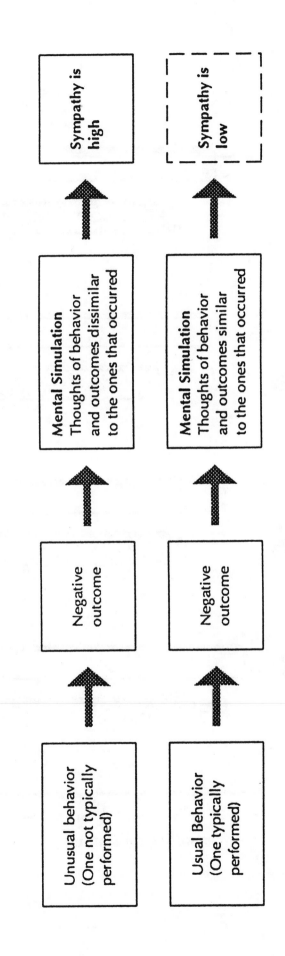

| Unusual behavior (One not typically performed) | → | Negative outcome | → | Mental Simulation Thoughts of behavior and outcomes dissimilar to the ones that occurred | → | Sympathy is high |
| Usual Behavior (One typically performed) | → | Negative outcome | → | Mental Simulation Thoughts of behavior and outcomes similar to the ones that occurred | → | Sympathy is low |

Mood and Social Judgements: A Field Study

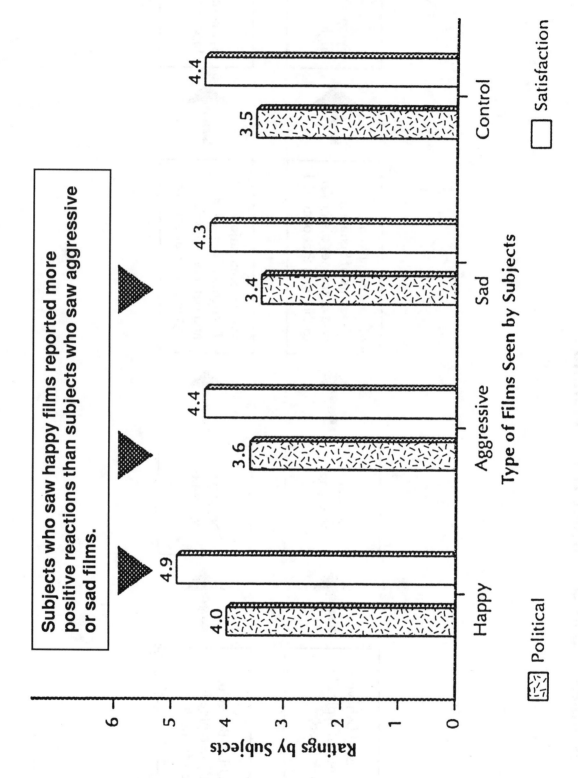

Subjects who saw happy films reported more positive reactions than subjects who saw aggressive or sad films.

Type of Films Seen by Subjects

Ratings by Subjects

Satisfaction

Political

T–3.3

T–3.4

How Cognition Sometimes Shapes Affect

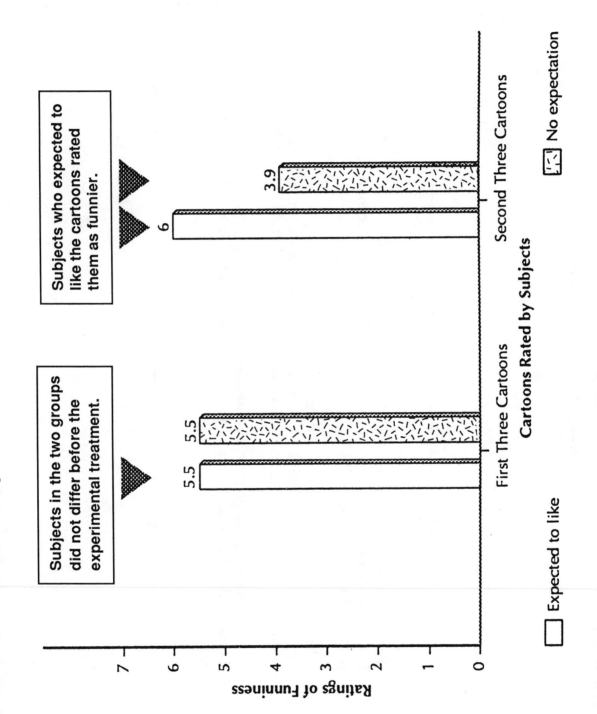

Subjects in the two groups did not differ before the experimental treatment.

Subjects who expected to like the cartoons rated them as funnier.

Ratings of Funniness

7
6
5
4
3
2
1
0

5.5 5.5

6

3.9

First Three Cartoons   Second Three Cartoons

Cartoons Rated by Subjects

☐ Expected to like   ☒ No expectation

Cognitive Dissonance Theory in a Nutshell

What is cognitive dissonance?
Feeling of *inconsistency* produced when two pieces of information held "in a person's head" are in conflict.

What is the source of this cognitive dissonance?
Usually caused by a conflict between our *belief* about something and the *knowledge* that we have performed a behavior contradictory to that belief.

How do people usually get rid of dissonance?
Since we don't like dissonance, we change our belief to make it consistent with our action.

The Forced Compliance Paradigm for Studying the Effects of Engaging in Attitude—Discrepant Behavior

Stage One: Obtain a sample of subjects who have a uniform attitude on some issue.

   A. One way is to use a "real world" issue where there is general agreement (example: a tuition increase uniformly opposed by students).

   B. Another strategy is to induce a "laboratory" attitude (example: have subjects perform a task that uniformly is perceived to be dull and boring).

Stage Two: Have subjects perform an attitude—discrepant action.

   A. Have them give a talk *favoring* tuition increase.

   B. Have them convince the "next subject" that the task is *fun and interesting.*

   Crucial Variable in Stage Two
   The amount of justification or reward provided for subject to perform attitude-discrepant action.

Stage Three: Measure the subject's attitude about the tuition increase or the task.

Dissonance: The Price of Inconsistency

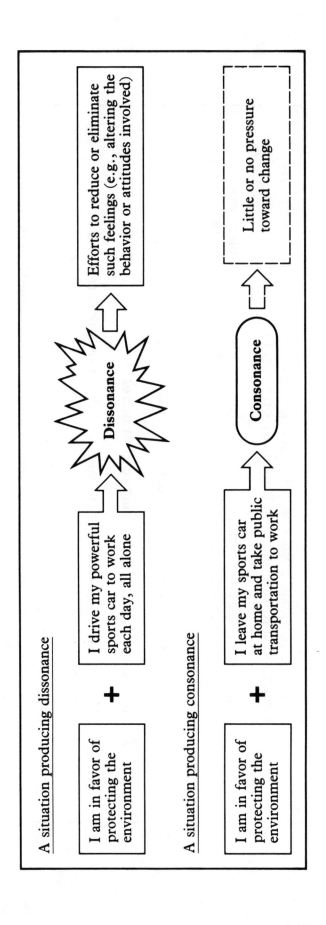

A situation producing dissonance

| I am in favor of protecting the environment | + | I drive my powerful sports car to work each day, all alone | → | **Dissonance** | → | Efforts to reduce or eliminate such feelings (e.g., altering the behavior or attitudes involved) |

A situation producing consonance

| I am in favor of protecting the environment | + | I leave my sports car at home and take public transportation to work | → | **Consonance** | → | Little or no pressure toward change |

Rewards and Forced-Compliance: Why "Less" Sometimes Leads to "More"

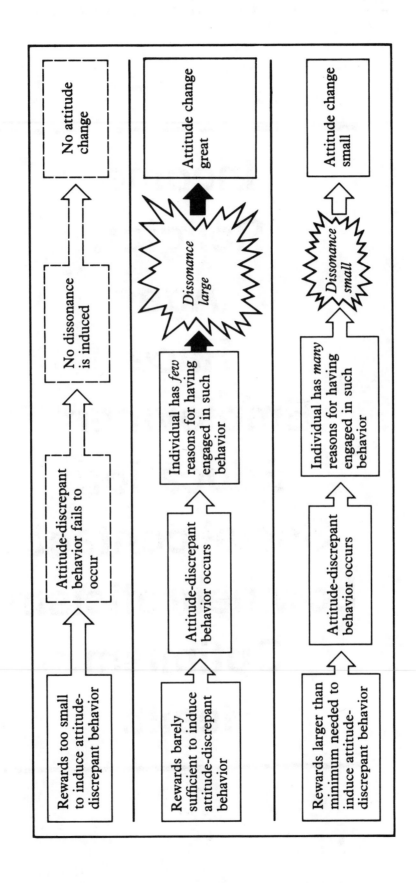

Income
Religion
Age
Race
Employment
Education
Social contact
Low neuroticism
Optimism
Health

Evolution of Beliefs in Traits

Up to the 1950's

Trait measures are "x-ray" to the mind

1960's through 1970's

Underlying assumption of traits,
behavioral consistency, undermined

1980's

Traits can predict when defined narrowly,
when individual differences in consistency considered
and when traits-situations jointly considered

Personality Development

Origin of Personality Characteristics		Personality Traits of an Individual		Behavior in Which Personality Variables are Reflected
Genetic factors Prenatal factors Childhood experiences Influence of culture, social class, race, religion, etc.	→	Development of stable personality characteristics involving emotional reactions, attitudes, motives, interests, beliefs, fears, desires	→	Responses to relevant internal and external stimulation consisting of needs, fantasies, thoughts, other people, situations, challenges, problems, etc.

Personality Measurement

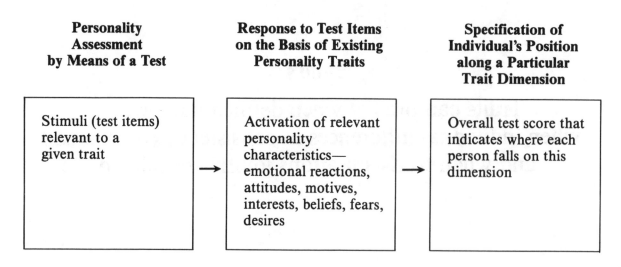

Personality Assessment by Means of a Test		Response to Test Items on the Basis of Existing Personality Traits		Specification of Individual's Position along a Particular Trait Dimension
Stimuli (test items) relevant to a given trait	→	Activation of relevant personality characteristics— emotional reactions, attitudes, motives, interests, beliefs, fears, desires	→	Overall test score that indicates where each person falls on this dimension

Interaction of "Strength of Situation" and the Personality Factor "Authoritarianism"

Experimental Conditions

Experimenter (E) Doesn't Pressure Subject (S) to Obey	**E Exerts Mild Pressure on S to Obey**	**E Exerts Strong Pressure on S to Obey**
Weak tendency to obey; strong correlation between measure of obedience and trait "Authoritarianism" (see Chapter 5)	Moderate tendency to obey; weak correlation between measure of obedience and trait "Authoritarianism"	Strong tendency to obey; no correlation between measure of obedience and trait "Authoritarianism"

Integrative Research using both Social and Personality Variables

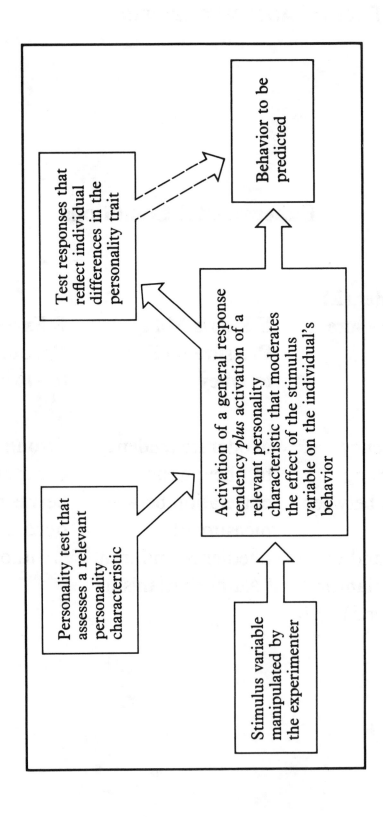

Five Basic Personality Dimensions	Characteristics of Those Who Are High versus Low on Each Dimension
Extraversion	talkative, frank, adventurous, and sociable *versus* silent, secretive, cautious, and reclusive
Agreeableness	good-natured, not jealous, gentle, and cooperative *versus* irritable, jealous, headstrong, and negativistic
Will to Achieve (or Conscientiousness)	fussy, responsible, scrupulous, and persevering *versus* careless, undependable, unscrupulous, and willing to quit
Emotional Stability (or Neuroticism)	poised, calm, composed, and not hypochondriacal *versus* nervous, anxious, excitable, and hypochondriacal
Openness to Experience (or Culture)	artistically sensitive, intellectual, polished, and imaginative *versus* insensitive, narrow, crude, and simple

Characteristics of Authoritarian Personality	Test Items Constructed to Measure Characteristic
Conventionalism	A person who has bad manners, habits, and breeding can hardly expect to get along with decent people.
Submission to a strong leader	Obedience and respect for authority are the most important virtues children should learn.
Aggression	Homosexuals are hardly better than criminals and ought to be severely punished.
Destruction and cynicism	The true American way of life is disappearing so fast that force may be necessary to preserve it.
Power and toughness	People can be divided into two distinct classes: the weak and the strong.
Anti-intraception	The businessman and the manufacturer are much more important to society than the artist and the professor.

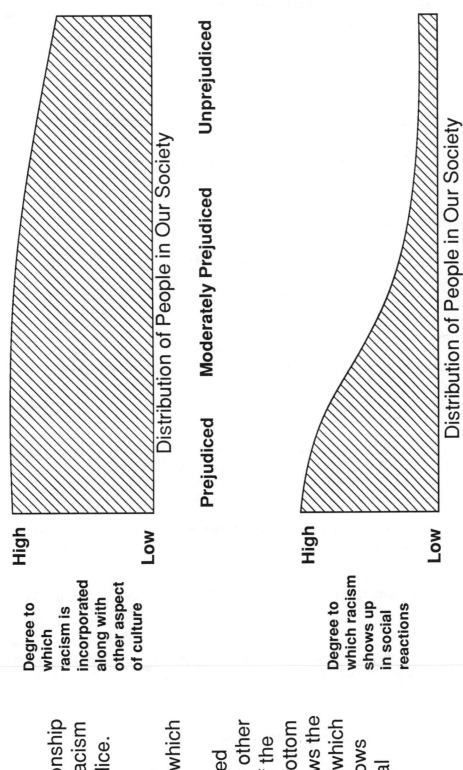

A Theory of the Relationship between Racism and Prejudice

The relationship between racism and prejudice. Top curve shows the degree to which racism is incorporated along with other aspects of the culture. Bottom curve shows the degree to which racism shows up in social reactions.

Degree to which racism is incorporated along with other aspect of culture

High

Low

Distribution of People in Our Society

Prejudiced   Moderately Prejudiced   Unprejudiced

Degree to which racism shows up in social reactions

High

Low

Distribution of People in Our Society

Prejudiced   Moderately Prejudiced   Unprejudiced

Projective (e.g., "evil figures" in TAT pictures are perceived to be minority persons)

Semantic Differential

"An American Indian"

good____:____:____:____:____:____:____:____:____:____bad

Anchored Scales

"Foreigners are generally less intelligent than Americans"

agree ____ ____ ____ ____ ____ ____ ____ ____ ____ disagree

Behavioral (e.g., when several chairs are present and a minority person is seated next to a wall, how closely to the minority person will a given person place her/his self, relative to when a nonminority person is seated next to the wall)

Check List (instruction: check all the groups listed below with whom you enjoy having close relations)

Stereotype Endorsement (instruction: check all of those statements that you would endorse)

Adjective Generation Technique (see prosocial chapter of this manual) (instruction: Write down five adjectives to describe a _____ person; e.g., female, Chinese, black, etc.)

Bogus Pipeline (explained on next transparency)

"Direct Intergroup Conflict":   White Californians turning Japanese-American business competitors in to authorities for incarceration during World War II.

"Social Categorization":   "Us" (the "Good Guys") versus "Them" (the "Bad Guys").

"Personality":   Authoritarians submit to a "leader" (e.g., Hitler) who will "save" them from the objects of their fear and loathing.

"Early Experience":   Media and parental reactions paint a picture of minorities as inferior.

The Tendency to View Outgroups as More Homogeneous than Ingroups: Empirical Evidence

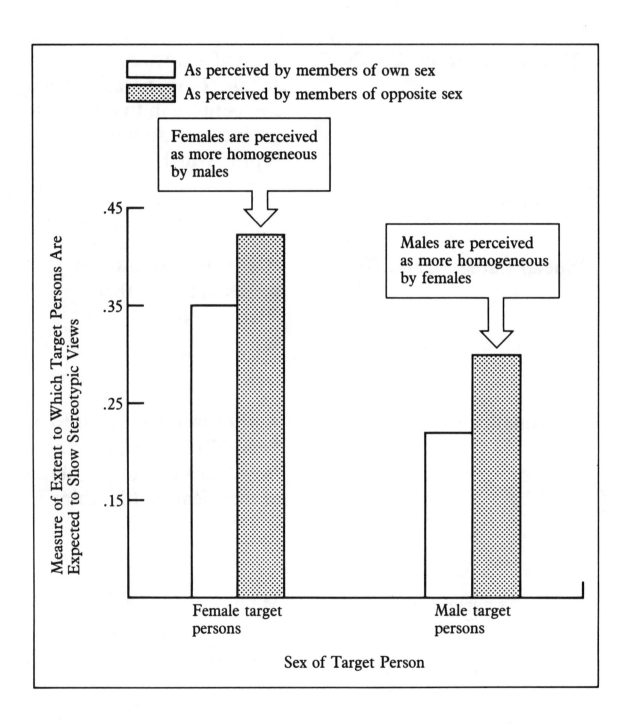

Intergroup Contact: How It Exerts Its Effects

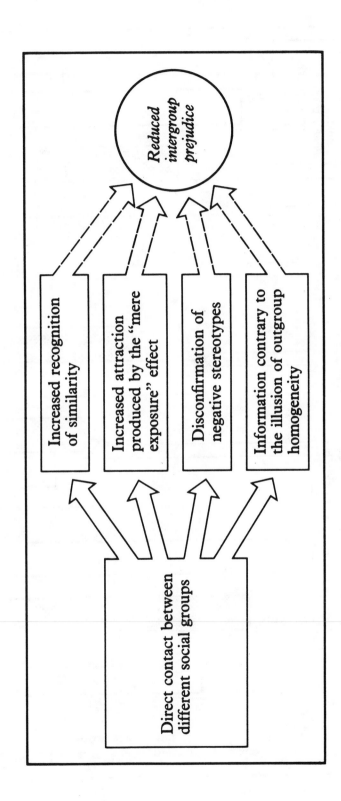

Male and Female Executives: The Stereotype that Failed

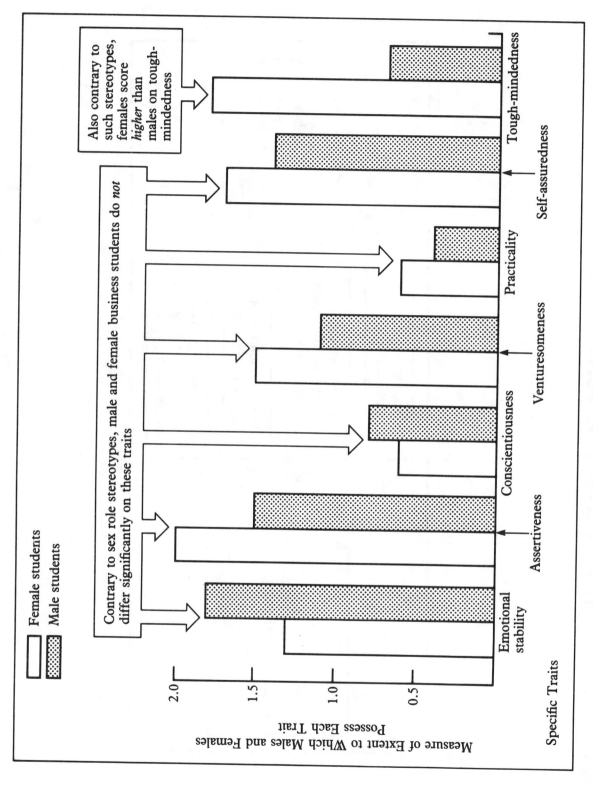

Female students

Male students

Also contrary to such stereotypes, females score *higher* than males on tough-mindedness

Contrary to sex role stereotypes, male and female business students do *not* differ significantly on these traits

Measure of Extent to Which Males and Females Possess Each Trait

2.0   1.5   1.0   0.5

Emotional stability · Assertiveness · Conscientiousness · Venturesomeness · Practicality · Self-assuredness · Tough-mindedness

Specific Traits

Agreements and Disagreements about African-Americans
(African-American % listed first)

Words used by about the Same % of each Sample *	Words used at differ-ent % by the sample	Words in one sample but in < 5% of the other	
corrupt (8,11)	smart[#] (27,9)	oppressed (14, <5)	fast (<5,6)
independent (10,10)	athletic (11,40)	beautiful (14,0)	obnoxious (0,7)
funny (6,10)	strong (27,6)	determined (8,0)	arrogant (<5,10)
friendly (10,11)	humorous (6,21)	educated (8,0)	emotional (6,0)
poor (6,6)	# Chi Sqrs significant at .03 or better	intelligent (13,<5)	misunder-stood (6,0)
*Chi Sqrs not significance		loud (<5,25)	
		mean (<5,9)	
		prejudiced (<5, 7)	
		musical (<5,7)	
		moody (0,6)	

Agreements and Disagreements about European-Americans (European-American % listed first)

Words used by About the Same % by each Sample

inventive (12,6)*

smart (32,19)

greedy (19,11)

educated (7,8)

rich (10,13)

*Chi Sqr not significant

Words used at Different % by the two Samples

competitive (19,6)

prejudiced (10,22)*

corrupt (6,41)

*Chi Sqr. significant at least at the .04 level

Words in one Sample, but in < 5% of the Other

egotistical (7,<5)

free (6,0)

happy (6,0)

kind (6,0)

mean (<5,16)

humorous (12,<5)

lazy (12,<5)

intelligent (10,<5)

racist (0,10)

selfish (0,11)

independent (12,<5)

arrogant (15,<5)

conceited (7<5)

friendly (15,<5)

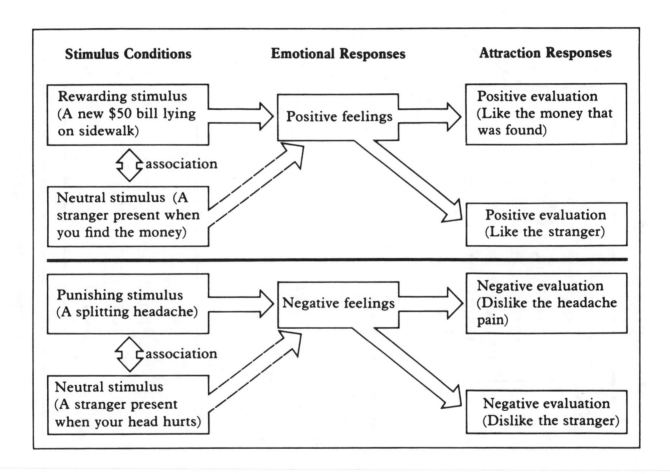

The Three-Factor Theory of Passionate Love

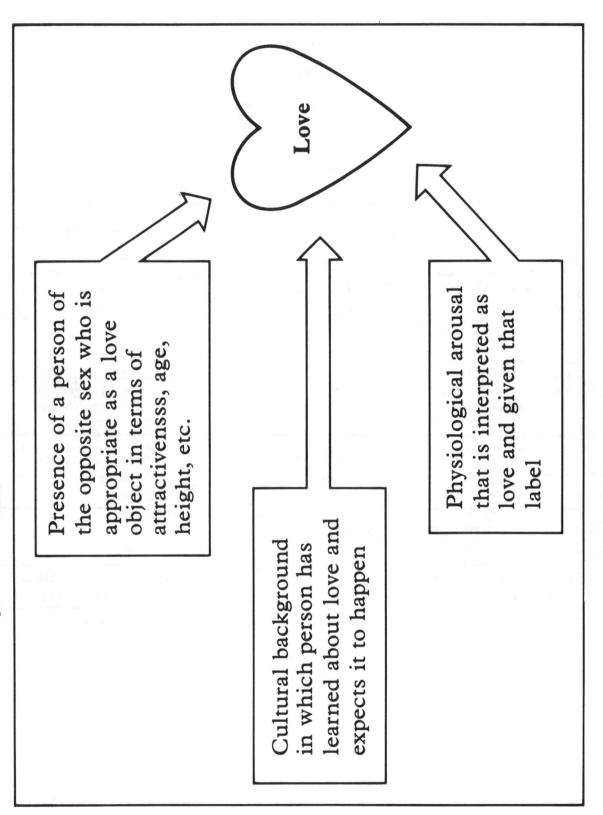

Presence of a person of the opposite sex who is appropriate as a love object in terms of attractivensss, age, height, etc.

Cultural background in which person has learned about love and expects it to happen

Physiological arousal that is interpreted as love and given that label

Love

The Reinforcement-Affect Theory: How Some Relationships May Start

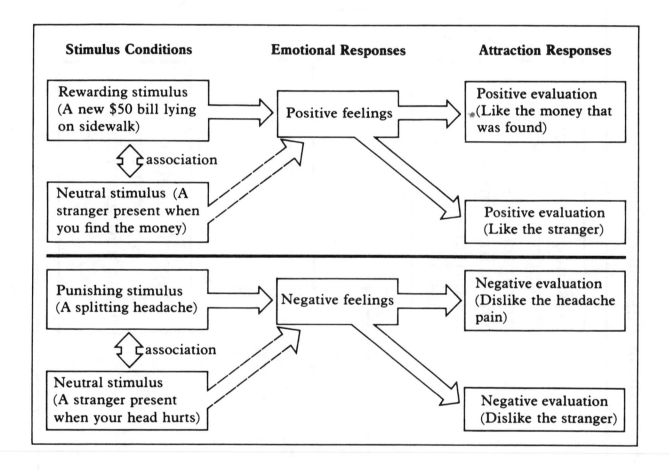

An Unromantic Explanation of Passionate Love

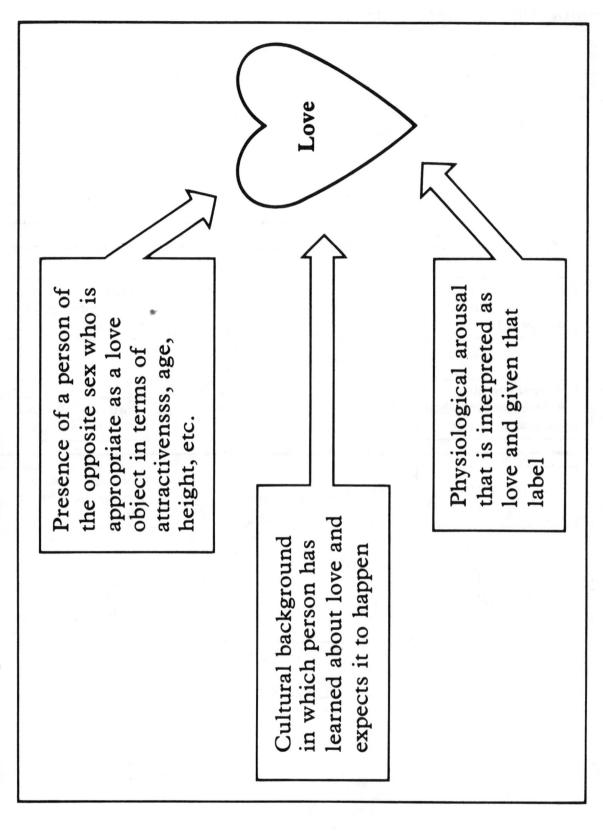

Presence of a person of the opposite sex who is appropriate as a love object in terms of attractivensss, age, height, etc.

Cultural background in which person has learned about love and expects it to happen

Physiological arousal that is interpreted as love and given that label

Love

Levinger's Theory that Relationships Pass through Five Stages from Beginning to End

Stage of Relationship	Positive Factors	Negative Factors
Initial Attraction	Propinquity and repeated exposure Positive emotions High affiliative need and friendship motivation	Absence of propinquity and repeated exposure Negative emotions Low affiliative need and friendship motivation
Building a Relationship	Equivalent physical attractiveness Similarity of attitudes and other characteristics Reciprocal positive evaluations	Nonequivalent physical attractiveness Dissimilarity of attitudes and other characteristics Reciprocal negative evaluations
Continuation	Seeking ways to maintain interest and variety Providing evidence of positive evaluation Absence of jealousy Perceived equity High level of mutual satisfaction	Falling into a rut and becoming bored Providing evidence of negative evaluation Jealousy Perceived inequity Low level of mutual satisfaction
Deterioration	Much time and effort invested in relationship Work at improvement of relationship Wait for improvement to occur	Little time and effort invested in relationship Decide to end relationship Wait for deterioration to continue
Ending	Existing relationship offers some rewards No alternative partners available Expect relationship to succeed Commitment to a continuing relationship	A new life appears to be the only acceptable solution Alternative partners available Expect relationship to fail Lack of commitment to a continuing relationship

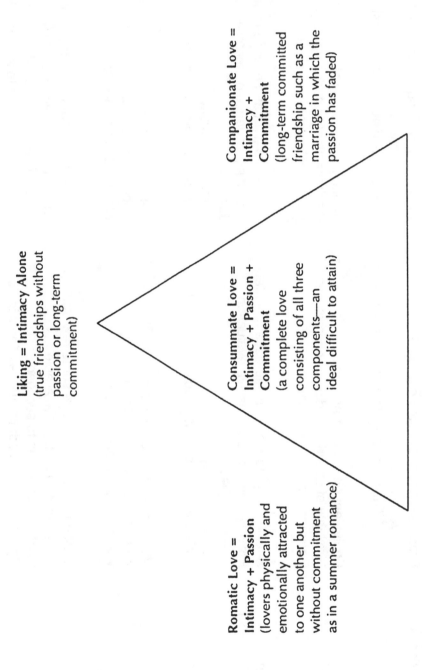

Sternberg's "Triangular Model of Love"

Liking = Intimacy Alone
(true friendships without passion or long-term commitment)

Companionate Love = Intimacy + Commitment
(long-term committed friendship such as a marriage in which the passion has faded)

Empty Love = Decision/Commitment Alone
(decision to love another without intimacy or passion)

Consummate Love = Intimacy + Passion + Commitment
(a complete love consisting of all three components—an ideal difficult to attain)

Romatic Love = Intimacy + Passion
(lovers physically and emotionally attracted to one another but without commitment as in a summer romance)

Fatuous Love = Passion + Commitment
(commitment based on passion but without time for intimacy to develop—shallow relationship such as a whirlwind courtship)

Infatuation = Passion Alone
(passionate, obsessive love at first sight without intimacy or commitment)

Relationships among Findings in the Lauer's Study of 351 Married Couples

Friendship

My spouse is my best friend

I like my spouse as a person

Commitment

Marriage is a long-term commitment.

Marriage is sacred.

I want the relationship to succeed.

An enduring marriage is important to social stability

Spouses in successful marriages say their relationship lasted because…

Similarity

We agree on aims and goals.

We agree on a philosophy of life.

We agree on how and how often to show affection.

We agree about our sex life.

Positive Affect

My spouse has grown more interesting

We laugh together

I am proud of may spouse's achievements

Behaviors That Upset Both Males and Females

In a relationship, partners who are unfaithful or abusive upset both males and females. In addition, several sex-specific behaviors are also upsetting. Explanations for these differences include a sociobiological emphasis on different reproductive strategies for the two sexes and a socialization emphasis on differences in what males and females learn about appropriate sex roles.

Behaviors That Upset Both Males and Females
Unfaithfulness
Physical abuse
Verbal abuse

Male Behaviors That Upset Females
Trying to demand or force sex
Ignoring a female's opinions and treating her as inferior or stupid
Hiding his emotions, acting tough, drinking or smoking excessively
Neglecting her, ignoring her, failing to say he loves her
Being thoughtless or rude, teasing her

Female Behaviors That Upset Males
Sexual rejection, being unresponsive
Moodiness, acting bitchy
Self-absorbed with her appearance and clothing

Source: Based on data in Buss, 1989.

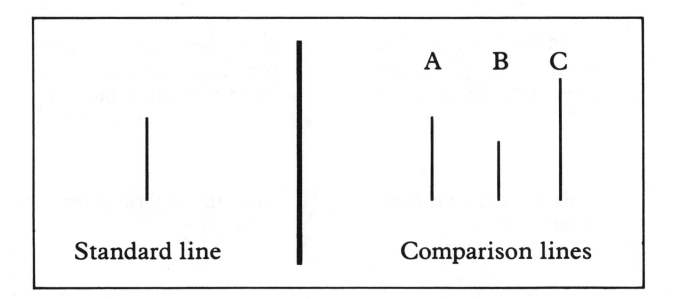

When the Sexes Might Differ in Conformity	When the Sexes Don't Differ in Conformity
when the issues on which pressure is applied more relevant to one sex	when the issues on which pressure is applied not more relevant to one sex
when the experimenter is male	when the experimenter is female
when objects of conformity pressure are under direct surveillance	when objects of conformity pressure are not under direct surveillance

"foot-in-the-door"	**"door-in-the-face"**	**"low balling"**
Self-perception: after first complying, sees self as "one who does that sort of thing"	**Self-presentation:** after first refusing, one looks bad by refusing again	**Commitment:** after agreeing, one becomes committed to agreement
View of helping: after first complying, sees helping in a more positive light	**Reciprocal concession:** after requester has "backed down," one feels need to reciprocate	**Unfulfilled obligation:** after agreeing one feels obligated to requester

The Tendency to Obey: Some Key Contributing Factors

High status of the authority figure

Belief among subordinates that the source of authority—not they—will be responsible for their actions

Absence of a clear-cut point for switching to disobedience

The gradual nature of many obedience situations (at first, following orders has only mild consequences; only later are more harmful effects produced)

A strong tendency to obey direct commands

The Social Influence Model (SIM)

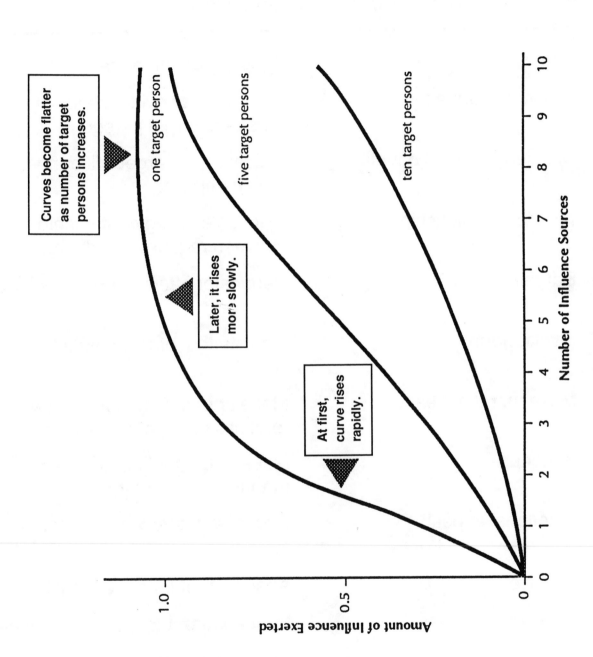

Curves become flatter as number of target persons increases.

Later, it rises more slowly.

At first, curve rises rapidly.

one target person

five target persons

ten target persons

Amount of Influence Exerted

Number of Influence Sources

Bisanz and Rule's Complete List of Means of Gaining Compliance

Name of Technique	Description
Ask	Simply present request
Present information	Offer facts or evidence to persuade target person
Mention personal benefits	Indicate how target will benefit from complying
Mention relationship	Mention existing relationship between requester and target
Bargain	Requester offers to do something in return
Invoke norm	Indicate that others would comply
Make moral appeal	Make appeal to a moral value (e.g., it's the right thing to do)
Butter up	Make target feel good in some manner (e.g., flattery)
Emotional appeal	Beg, plead, throw a tantrum, sulk
Criticize	Attack target for not complying
Deceive	Mislead target to gain compliance
Threaten	Threaten target to gain compliance
Force	Use force to gain compliance

Good Samaritan Roadmap

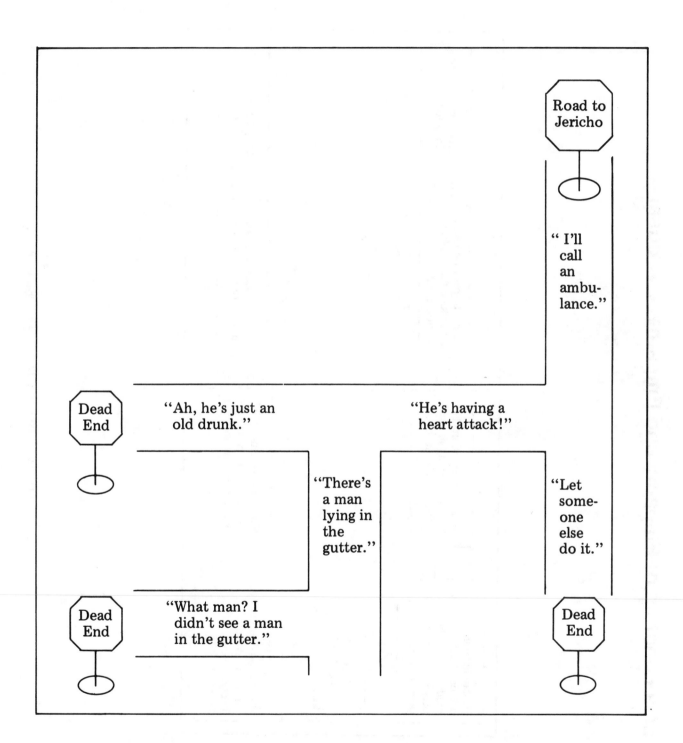

Road to Jericho

" I'll call an ambulance."

Dead End

"Ah, he's just an old drunk."

"He's having a heart attack!"

"There's a man lying in the gutter."

"Let someone else do it."

Dead End

"What man? I didn't see a man in the gutter."

Dead End

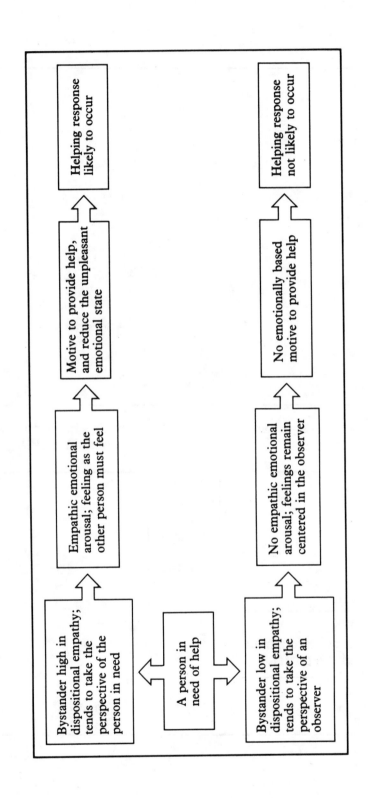

T-10.2

Helping as a Function of Empathy and Empathetic Arousal

Bystander high in dispositional empathy; tends to take the perspective of the person in need

Empathic emotional arousal; feeling as the other person must feel

Motive to provide help, and reduce the unpleasant emotional state

Helping response likely to occur

A person in need of help

Bystander low in dispositional empathy; tends to take the perspective of an observer

No empathic emotional arousal; feelings remain centered in the observer

No emotionally based motive to provide help

Helping response not likely to occur

Six Levels of Helpfulness-Unhelpfulness

Analysis of responses to specific emergency situations suggests that the extent to which bystanders help or fail to help can be categorized as falling at six levels. In the example here, subjects were asked to imagine themselves overhearing a woman saying that she is feeling ill, dizzy, and anxious. The subjects were asked what, if anything, they would do in this situation. Their responses ranged from a direct intervention with a plan about what to do on one extreme to a refusal to help based on attributions about the woman and a rationalization for not doing anything.

Six levels of helpfulness–unhelpfulness

Helpful Responses

1. Direct Intervention with a Plan for Helping

"I'll give her my seat, and offer to get her a glass of water or wait with her."

2. General Help

"I'll go over and ask if she's okay."

3. Indirect Help or Reporting the Incident

"I'll tell someone at the hotel desk that the woman on the phone needs assistance."

4. Conditional Help

"If she walks around where I'm sitting and if she looks really sick and wants my help, then I guess I'll help her."

Unhelpful Responses

5. No Help or Interaction

"I think I'll read this magazine."

6. Refusal to Help Along with an Attribution or Rationalization

"I'm not going to help her. The information probably isn't important anyway."

Source: Based on data in Lang, 1987.

Components of Altruistic Personality

In an attempt to identify the factors that make up the altruistic personality, investigators compared citizens who witnessed a traffic accident and provided first aid to the victim with citizens who witnessed such an accident and did not provide first aid. As indicated here, five personality characteristics were found to differentiate the two groups. Together these characteristics identify altruistic individuals.

Components of the altruistic personality

Individuals Who Administered First Aid after a Traffic Accident	Individuals Who Failed to Administer First Aid
Were higher in internal locus of control	Were lower in internal locus of control
Believed more strongly in a just world	Believed less strongly in a just world
Felt more socially responsible (were interested in public matters and involved in the community; felt a sense of duty)	Felt less socially responsible
Had higher empathy component in self-concept.	Had lower empathy component in self-concept
Were less egocentric	Were more egocentric

Source: Based on data in Bierhoff, Klein, & Kramp, 1991.

Motivations Underlying AIDS Volunteerism

Those who volunteer to help in the AIDS epidemic do so on the basis of five different motivations. Thus, the same overt behavior can satisfy quite different needs. Those who recruit volunteers do best to aim different kinds of recruiting messages to those whose motives differ. Interestingly, recruits who continue such work over time are more likely than those who quit to be motivated by the "self-centered" motives—enhancement of self-esteem or desire for personal development.

Motivations underlying AIDS volunteerism

Motivation for Volunteering to Help in the AIDS Epidemic

1. Personal Values	"Because of my humanitarian obligation to help others"
2. Desire to Increase Understanding	"Because I want to learn how people cope with AIDS"
3. Community Concern	"Because of my concern and worry about the gay community"
4. Personal Development	"I want to challenge myself and test my skills"
5. Enhancement of Self-Esteem	"I want to feel better about myself"

Source: Based on data in Snyder & Omoto, 1992.)

1. Uninvited pressure for sexual favors
2. Uninvited and deliberate touching
3. Uninvited letters, phone calls, or materials of a sexual nature
4. Uninvited sexually suggestive looks or gestures
5. Uninvited pressure for dates
6. Uninvited sexual teasing, jokes, remarks, or questions

Aggression as Innate

Freud — "death instinct" redirected toward others

Lorenz — "fighting instinct" disperses populations over wide areas maximizing use of available resources

Sociobiology — aggression a part of the evolutionary process because it was adaptive

Drive Theories

External conditions such as frustration give rise to motive to hurt

Social Learning Theories

Aggression is viewed as a learned social behavior that can be altered

Possible Causes	Possible Cures
Frustration	Disapproving commentary about T.V. violence
Verbal attack	Nonaggressive models
Physical attack	Punishment
Models of aggression	Catharsis
Heightened arousal	Mild sexual arousal
Strong sexual arousal	Nonhostile humor
Alcohol	Generating empathy
Aggressive cues	Marijuana
Audiences	
Crowding	
Heat	
Personality	
Genes	
Gender	
Hostile humor	

Media Violence: Mechanisms Underlying the Effects

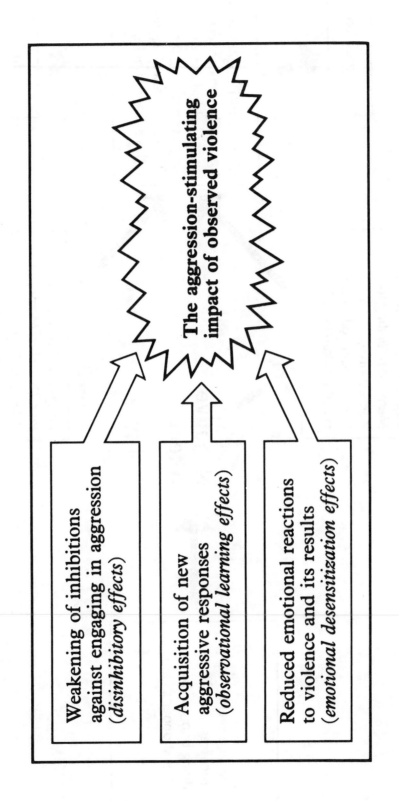

Aggression according to the Neoassociationists

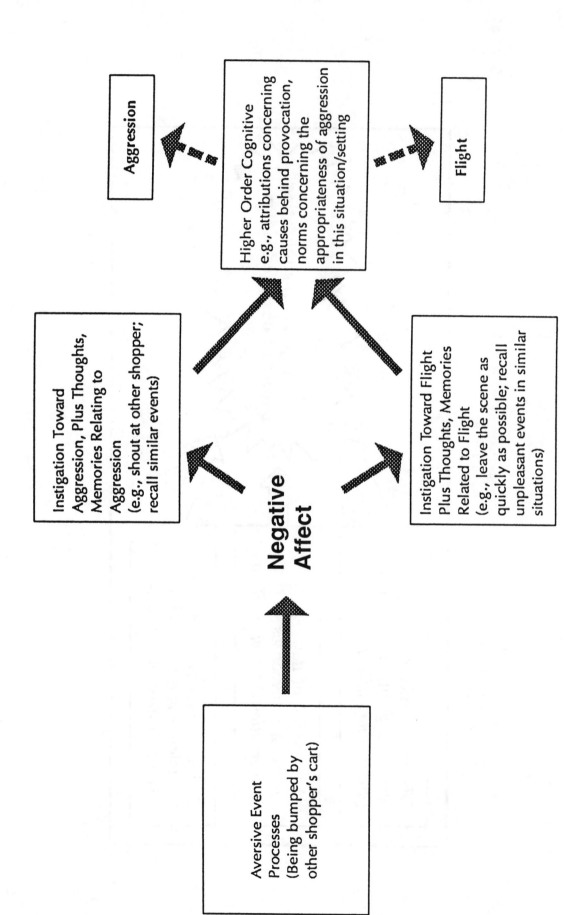

Aversive Event Processes (Being bumped by other shopper's cart)

↓

Negative Affect

Instigation Toward Aggression, Plus Thoughts, Memories Relating to Aggression (e.g., shout at other shopper; recall similar events)

Instigation Toward Flight Plus Thoughts, Memories Related to Flight (e.g., leave the scene as quickly as possible; recall unpleasant events in similar situations)

Higher Order Cognitive e.g., attributions concerning causes behind provocation, norms concerning the appropriateness of aggression in this situation/setting

Aggression

Flight

The Effects of Violent and Nonviolent Pornography on Males' Aggression toward Females

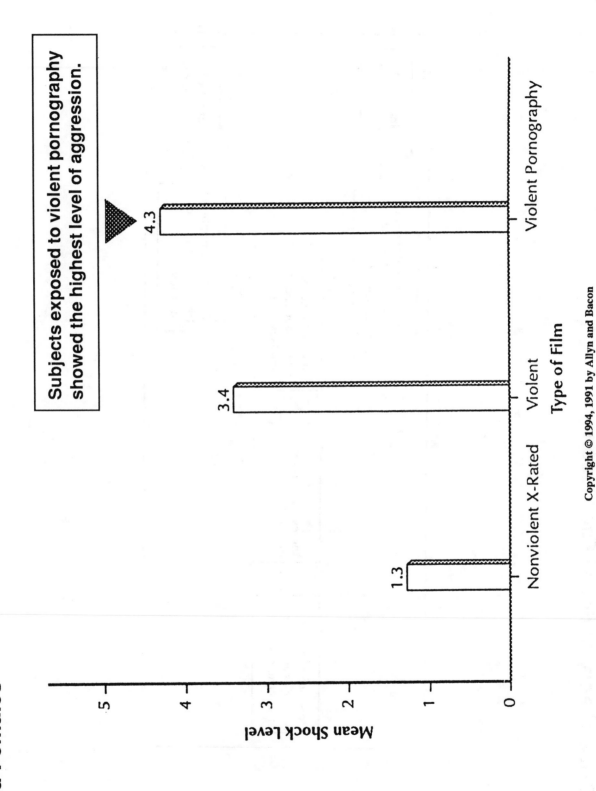

Subjects exposed to violent pornography showed the highest level of aggression.

Mean Shock Level

5
4
3
2
1
0

Nonviolent X-Rated   Violent   Violent Pornography

Type of Film

1.3

3.4

4.3

The Drive Theory of Social Facilitation

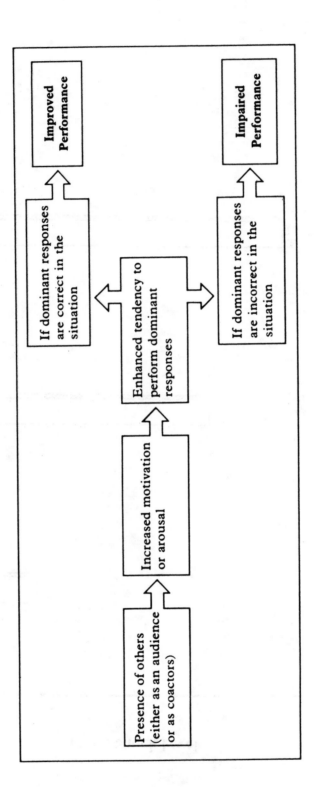

The Distraction—Conflict Theory of Social Facilitation

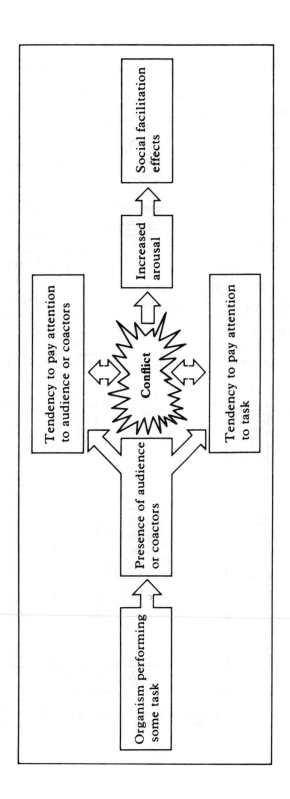

The Contingency Model of Leadership Effectiveness   T-12.3

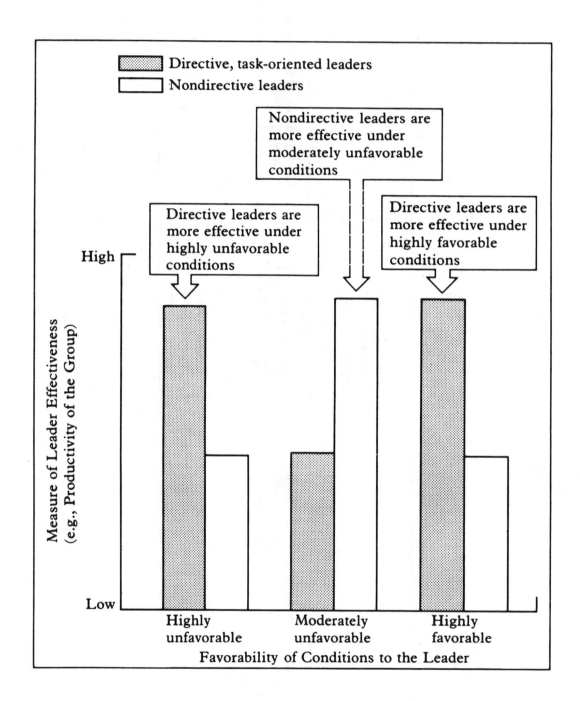

Environmental Behavior Can Be Changed by Legislation

legislation regulating one aspect of environmental behavior: the bottle bill

compliance with the law based on monetary rewards and acceptance of social norms

new behavior becomes habitual

attitudes about the bottle bill become more favorable, a shift based on the desire for consistency

attitudes generalize, resulting in positive views about other environmental issues

Three Gases Contributing to the Greenhouse Effect

Type of Gas	Amount of Contribution to Greenhouse Effect	What Must Be Done to Stabilize Amount of the Gas in the Atmosphere
carbon dioxide	50%	reduce emissions by 50 to 80 percent through changes in behavior and in technology
methane	25%	reduce emissions by ruminants (cattle, sheep, etc.) through changes in their diets
chlorofluorocarbons	25%	use of this gas must be totally banned

Common Stressful Events among College Students	Common Stressful Events among Others

High Levels of Stress (71 to 100 points)

unwed pregnancy	death of spouse
father in unwed pregnancy	death of parent
	divorce

Moderate Levels of Stress (31 to 70 points)

parents divorce	death of close relative
flunking out	death of close friend
loss of financial aid	jail term
failing important course	major injury or illness
sexual difficulties	marriage
argument with romantic partner	loss of job
on academic probation	increased workload on job
change of major	
finding a new love interest	

Low Levels of Stress (1 to 30 points)

outstanding achievement	minor violations of the law
enrolled for first semester	
conflict with instructor	
lower grades than expected	
transfer to a different college	
change in social activities	
change in sleeping habits	
change in eating habits	

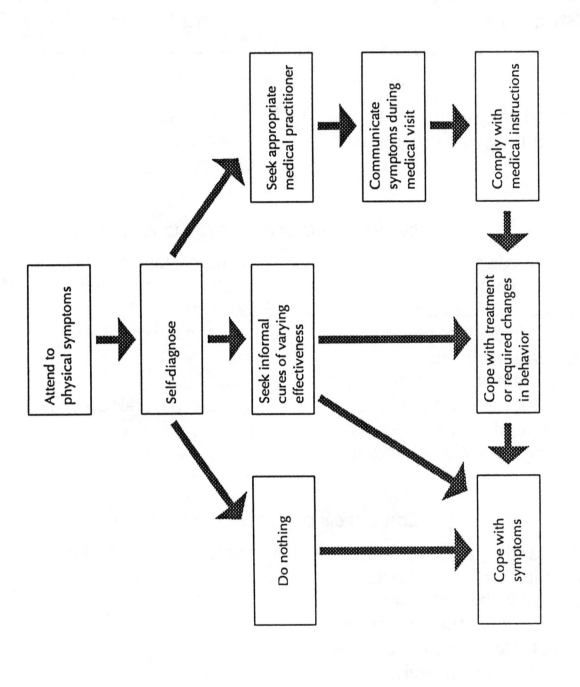

Decisions and Choices to Make when the Symptoms of Illness Develop

Attend to physical symptoms

Self-diagnose

Seek appropriate medical practitioner

Communicate symptoms during medical visit

Comply with medical instructions

Seek informal cures of varying effectiveness

Do nothing

Cope with treatment or required changes in behavior

Cope with symptoms

Concerns About Technological Hazards

Surveys indicate that people are concerned about the dangerous effects of technology on our health and safety. Scientific experts at the Environmental Protection Agency agree that hazards exist, but their assessments tend not to match those of the general public. People in general seem to worry most about immediate, short-term problems, while the scientists are more concerned about future, long-term problems.

Concerns about technological hazards: The public versus the experts

	Perceptions of the General Public	Perceptions of Experts
Highest Concerns	Contaminated drinking water Storage of toxic chemicals Cancer-causing chemicals	Global climate change Species extinction and loss of biological diversity Soil erosion and deforestation
Moderate Concerns	Pesticide residue in food Air pollution Nuclear power plant accidents	Herbicides and pesticides Pollution of surface water Acid rain
Low Concerns	Car accidents Transport of explosives Food preservatives	Oil spills Groundwater pollution Escape of radioactive materials

Source: Based on data in Pilisuk & Acredolo, 1988, and Stevens, 1991a.

High Level Versus Low Level Goals in Life

Personal strivings are the characteristic recurring goals that a person is trying to accomplish in his or her life. People differ in whether they strive for relatively difficult, abstract goals or relatively easy, concrete ones. Those who emphasize high-level strivings experience more psychological stress (because they can't meet their goals) but less physical illness (because their commitment increases hardiness). Those who emphasize low-level strivings experience less emotional discomfort (because they can reach their goals) but more illness (because of a lack of commitment).

TABLE 13.2 High-level versus low-level goals in life

High-Level, Abstract Strivings	Low-Level, Concrete Strivings
I want to deepen my relationship with God.	I want to look well-groomed and clean-cut.
I want to be totally honest.	I want to be funny and make others laugh.
I want to be a fun person to be around.	I want to look attentive and not bored in class.
I want to compete against myself rather than against others.	I want to be organized and neat—clean my room and make my bed.
I want to increase my knowledge of the world.	I want to work hard or at least look like I'm working hard.

Source: Based on data in Emmons, 1992.

Unfair Punishment: Different Sets of Biases   T–14.1

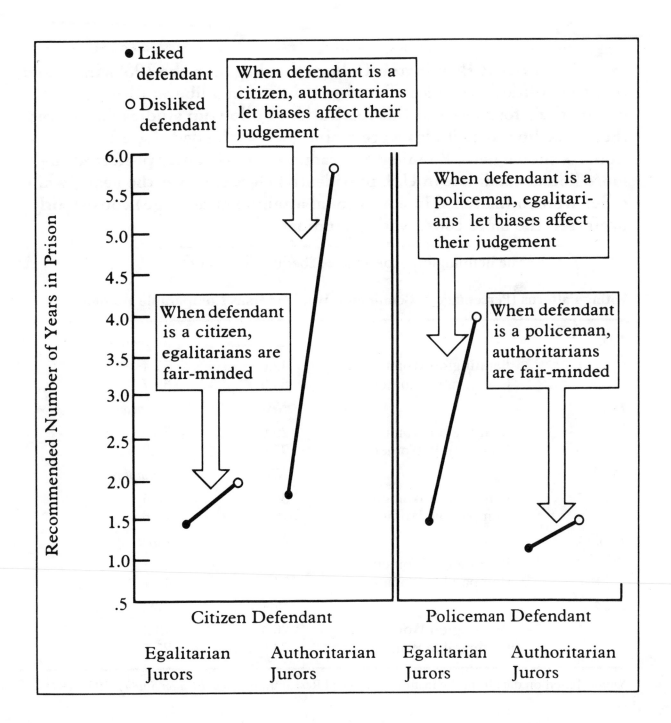

The Bennington Experience

Research at Bennington College that began in the 1930s indicated that the political attitudes of students shifted in a liberal direction during their four years at this institution. Follow-up studies discovered that these liberal attitudes were maintained in the decades after graduation. As shown here, Bennington graduates consistently preferred the more liberal candidate in U.S. presidential elections over the years, while other women (matched in educational attainment and age) consistently preferred the more conservative candidate.

The Bennington experience: Liberals for a lifetime

Voting Patterns (Percentages): Bennington Women versus Comparable Women

1952		*Eisenhower*	*Stevenson*
	Bennington Women	42.6	57.4
	Comparable Women	64.3	35.7
1960		*Nixon*	*Kennedy*
	Bennington Women	26.0	74.0
	Comparable Women	75.0	25.0
1968		*Nixon*	*Humphrey*
	Bennington Women	32.9	66.5
	Comparable Women	79.1	18.6
1976		*Ford*	*Carter*
	Bennington Women	31.2	68.8
	Comparable Women	54.9	45.1
1984		*Reagan*	*Mondale*
	Bennington Women	26.4	73.3
	Comparable Women	73.0	25.7

Source: Based on data from the Institute for Social Research, *National Election Studies, 1952–1984.*

What is Important in Selecting a Jury

Before a trial begins, attorneys take part in a jury selection process in which they look for certain positive and negative characteristics and ask various questions in an effort to decide which prospective jurors should be retained and which should be excused. When attorneys were asked to indicate the most important characteristics and the voir dire (to speak truthfully) questions they most often ask, these were the results.

What do attorneys seek in selecting a jury?

**Characteristics Attorneys Say
Are Important in Jury Selection**

Intelligence
Age
Appearance
Occupation
Open-mindedness
Gender
Attentiveness
Impressibility
Race

**Voir Dire Questions Attorneys Say
They Ask Most Often**

What is your attitude about this kind of crime?
What is your general reaction to police officers?
How much have you heard about this case in the media?
Were you ever the victim of this kind of crime?
How do you feel about someone who has been arrested?
Do you have any racial bias?
Have any of your acquaintances ever been arrested or convicted
Do you have any relationship with any of the individuals connected with this case?

Source: Based on data from Olczak, Kaplan, & Penrod, 1991.

Equity and Inequity in Social Exchange

Equity is perceived to exist

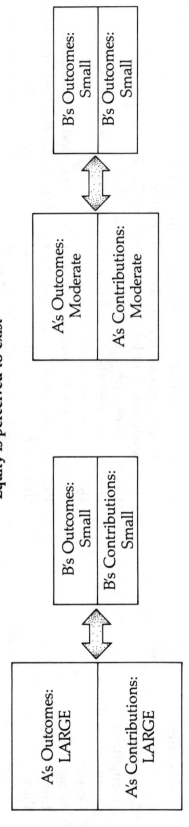

Inequity is perceived to exist

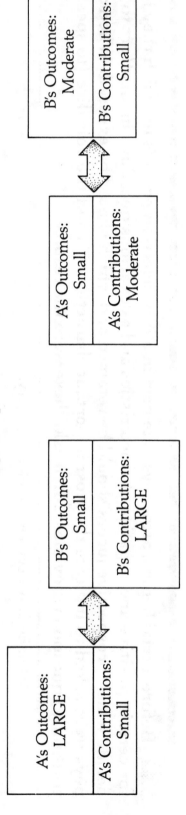

Questionnaire Measure Job Satisfaction

The items shown here are similar to those used on two popular measures of job satisfaction. (Please note: the items shown are not identical to ones on the actual questionnaires.)

TABLE 14.4 Questionnaires for measuring job satisfaction

Job Description Index (JDI)

Enter "Yes," "No," or "?" for each description or word below.

Work itself:

_____ Routine

_____ Satisfactory

_____ Good

Promotions:

_____ Dead-end job

_____ Few promotions

_____ Good opportunity for promotion

Minnesota Satisfaction Questionnaire (MSQ)

Indicate the extent to which you are satisfied with each aspect of your present job. Enter one number next to each aspect.

1 = Not at all satisfied

2 = Not satisfied

3 = Neither satisfied nor dissatisfied

4 = Satisfied

5 = Extremely satisfied

_____ Utilization of your abilities

_____ Authority

_____ Company policies and practices

_____ Independence

_____ Supervision, human relations

Exercises

Social psychologists have found in their research that separation intensifies romantic attraction. In other words, there seems to be wisdom in the old saying, "Absence makes the heart grow fonder."

In a sentence or two, why do you suppose this is true?

Does this finding seem surprising to you?

_____yes   _____no

Social psychologists have found in their research that separation weakens romantic attraction. There seems to be wisdom in the old saying, "Out of sight, out of mind."

In a sentence or two, why do you suppose this is true?

Does this finding seem surprising to you?

_____yes   _____no

EXERCISE 4

Descriptions of Studies
(from Wilson and Donnerstein, 1976)

1.   Experimenters, walking singly or in pairs, ask politely for either 10 cents or 20 cents from passersby, sometimes offering an explanation for why they need the money   (Latane, 1970)

2.   The experimenter comes to a home, says that he has misplaced the address of a friend who lives nearby, and asks to use the phone. If the party admits him, he pretends to make the call   (Milgram, 1970)

3.   Automobiles, parked on streets, look as if they were abandoned. (License plates are removed and hoods are raised.)   Experimenters hide in nearby buildings and film people who have any contact with the cars   (Zimbardo, 1969).

4.   Two researchers visit shoe stores at times when there are more customers than sales clerks in the store. One of the researchers is wearing a shoe with a broken heel.   She rejects whatever new shoes the sales clerk shows her.   The other researcher, posing as a friend of the bogus customer, surreptitiously takes notes on the sales clerk's behavior   (Schaps, 1972)

5.   Letters, stamped and addressed to fictitious organizations at the same post office box number, are dropped in various locations, as if they were lost on the way to being mailed. Some are placed under automobile windshield wipers with a penciled note saying "found near car"   (Milgram, 1969).

EXERCISE 4

6. People sitting alone on park benches are asked to be interviewed by an experimenter who gives the name of a fictitious survey research organization that he claims to represent. At the beginning of the interview, the experimenter asks a person sitting nearby, who is actually a confederate, if he would mind answering the questions at the same time. The confederate responds with opinions that are opposite those of the subject and makes demeaning remarks about the subject's answers; for example, "that's ridiculous," "that's just the sort of thing you'd expect to hear in this park" (Abelson and Miller, 1967)

7. A person walking with a cane pretends to collapse in a subway car. "Stage blood" trickles from his mouth. If someone approaches the bogus victim, he allows the party to help him to his feet. If no one approaches before the train slows to a stop, another experimenter, posing as a passenger, pretends to help and both leave the train (Piliavin and Piliavin, 1972).

8. Housewives are phoned. The caller names a fictitious consumers' group that he claims to represent and interviews them about the soap products they use for a report in a "public service publication," which is also fictitious. Several days later the experimenter calls again and asks if the housewives would allow five or six men into their homes to enumerate and classify their household products for a report in their publication. If the party agrees, the caller says he is just collecting names of willing people at present and that she will be contacted if it is decided to use her in the survey. No one is contacted again (Freedman and Fraser, 1966).

EXERCISE 5

1. A study was conducted to investigate the hypothesis that watching televised violence increases aggression in children. Fifty 4-year olds were randomly assigned to watch either a violent or a non-violent television program. After watching the program the children were observed while they engaged in 30 minutes of free play. An observer watched for aggressive acts and recorded all such acts that occurred.

2. A pharmaceutical compay hired a team of researchers to study the effectiveness of a new drug for relieving depression. The researchers identified a group of psychiatric patients who were experiencing chronic depression and randomly assigned half of them to receive the drug and half to receive a placebo. One month later the drug group had improved much more than the placebo group, and the pharmaceutical company announced it had found a new anti-depressant drug.

3. It was hypothesized that people have a desire to be with other people when they are in a fear-arousing situation. To test this hypothesis an experimenter randomly assigned 50 subjects to either a low or a high fear group. The low fear group was told they would be shocked but that it would be only a small tingle and that it definitely would not hurt. The high fear group was told they would be shocked and that the shock would be quite painful. Each group of subjects was then told they had to wait while the equipment was being prepared and that they could wait in a room by themselves or with others. The number of subjects who chose to wait alone and to wait with others was recorded by the experimenter.

4. An investigator wanted to determine how massed versus distributed practice affects learning. To accomplish this she developed a list of nonsense syllables and had subjects learn these under two different conditions. Twenty subjects practiced the list for twenty minutes without any break (massed practice), while another twenty subjects practiced for four five-minute periods with a two minute break between each period (distributed practice). The number of nonsense syllables correctly recalled at the end of practice was recorded for each subject.

5. An educator was interested in identifying the most successful teaching technique for his school system. He identified three schools that taught in the traditional manner and another three schools that taught in a new experimental manner. At the end of the school year, he administered an achievement test to all the children in these schools.

EXERCISE 5A

Critical thinking questions:

1. What if the observer recording the children's aggressive acts becomes fatigued or bored during the course of the 30-minute sessions? Would it matter that the observer's criterion as to what represents an aggressive act changes over the course of the 30-minute sessions?

2. Assume that "to avoid confusion" the researchers decided to have the actual drug administered by one psychiatric nurse and the placebo by another nurse. Is this a good idea? Why or why not?

3. Some subjects in the high fear condition might choose to discontinue their participation in the experiment after hearing about the painful shocks, and ethical guidelines require that the experimenter release them. Would the experimental procedure be compromised if 15% of the high-fear subjects dropped out, but none of the low-fear subjects did so?

4. The experimenter allowed distributed-practice subjects to "do whatever they wanted" during the two-minute rest periods, and many of them mentally rehearsed the nonsense syllables during this time. Is this a problem? If so, what changes are needed to correct for it?

5. Obviously, the educator could not randomly assign the children to attend the various schools. Also, he was not allowed to decide which teachers or schools would use each technique. What problems are caused by: 1) not being able to randomly assign children to the schools? 2) having teachers "choose" which teaching technique to use?

EXERCISE 1

A STORY FROM LONG AGO

Once upon a time, a husband and wife lived together in a part of the city separated by a river from the places of employment, shopping, and entertainment. The husband had to work nights. Each evening he left his wife and took the ferry to work, returning in the morning.

The wife soon tired of this arrangement. Restless and lonely, she would take the next ferry into town each evening and develop relationships with a series of lovers. Anxious to preserve her marriage, she always returned home before her husband. In fact, her relationships were always limited. When they threatened to become too intense, she would precipitate a quarrel with her current lover and begin a new relationship.

One night she caused such a quarrel with a man we will call Lover I. He slammed the door in her face, and she started back to the ferry. Suddenly she realized that she had forgotten to bring money for her return fare. She swallowed her pride and returned to Lover I's apartment to borrow the fare. After all, she did have to get home. But Lover I was vindictive and angry because of the quarrel. He slammed the door on his former lover, leaving her with no money. She remembered that a previous lover, whom we shall call Lover II, lived just a few doors away. Surely he would give her the ferry fare. However, Lover II was still so hurt from their old quarrel that he, too, refused her the money.

Now the hour was late and the woman was getting desperate. She rushed down to the ferry and pleaded with the ferryboat captain. He knew her as a regular customer. She asked if he could let her ride free and if she could pay the next night. But the captain insisted that rules were rules and that he could not let her ride without paying the fare.

Dawn would soon be breaking, and her husband would be returning from work. The woman remembered that there was a free bridge about a mile further on.   But the road to the bridge was a dangerous one, known to be frequented by highwaymen. Nonetheless, she had to get home, so she took the road. On the way a highwayman stepped out of the bushes and demanded her money. She told him she had none. He seized her. In the ensuing tussle, the highwayman stabbed the woman, and she died.

Thus ends our story. There have been six characters: Husband, Wife, Lover I, Lover II, Ferryboat Captain and Highwayman. Please list, in descending order of responsibility for this woman's death, all the characters. In other words, the one most responsible is listed first; the next most responsible, second; and so forth.

EXERCISE 2

INSTRUCTIONS: Your task is to imagine yourself in the situations below and to rate your action in each situation. Use the following 1 to 5 scale to rate each action.

1--Action was exclusively due to my characteristics

2--Action was mainly due to my characteristics

3--Action was equally due to my characteristics and to the situation

4--Action was mainly due to the situation

5--Action was exclusively due to the situation

1. I was at a restaurant and received the wrong meal. I sat quietly and ate it without complaining. ____
2. I just received an A on a term paper. ____
3. I had a fight with one of my best friends. ____
4. I lied on a job application. ____
5. I was walking across the street and saw an accident happen, so I went over to see if I could help. ____
6. Someone was visiting me, but I said I had to study and I asked my visitor to leave. ____
7. Someone asked me for help moving into a new apartment on Saturday, and I lied and said I had other plans. ____
8. My least favorite professor said something stupid in class, and I laughed out loud, although nobody else did. ____
9. I entered a contest, solved a puzzle, and won $500. ____
10. I gave $100 of the contest winnings to a student aid fund on campus. ____
11. I volunteered to coach a children's athletic team in a local elementary school. ____
12. I found a wallet with $50 on the street and gave it to the police. ____
13. I was caught speeding on the way home last week and received a ticket and $50 fine. ____
14. My professor singled me out as an excellent studentand offered me a job in the department. ____

EXERCISE 2A

INSTRUCTIONS: Your task is to imagine a particular friend in the situations below and to rate your friend's action in each situation. Use the following 1 to 5 scale to rate each action.

1--Action was exclusively due to my friend's characteristics

2--Action was mainly due to my friend's characteristics

3--Action was equally due to my friend's characteristics and to the situation

4--Action was mainly due to the situation

5--Action was exclusively due to the situation

1. My friend was at a restaurant and received the wrong meal. My friend sat quietly and ate it without complaining. ＿＿＿＿
2. My friend just received an A on a term paper. ＿＿＿＿
3. My friend had a fight with one of his/her best friends. ＿＿＿＿
4. My friend lied on a job application. ＿＿＿＿
5. My friend was walking across the street and saw an accident happen, so my friend went over to see if he/she could help. ＿＿＿＿
6. My friend had someone visiting, but my friend said he/she had to study and asked the visitor to leave. ＿＿＿＿
7. Someone asked my friend for help moving into a new apartment on Saturday, and my friend lied and said he/she had other plans. ＿＿＿＿
8. My friend's least favorite professor said something stupid in class, and my friend laughed out loud, although nobody else did. ＿＿＿＿
9. My friend entered a contest, solved a puzzle, and won $500. ＿＿＿＿
10. My friend gave $100 of the contest winnings to a student aid fund on campus. ＿＿＿＿
11. My friend volunteered to coach a children's athletic team in a local elementary school. ＿＿＿＿
12. My friend found a wallet with $50 on the street and gave it to the police. ＿＿＿＿
13. My friend was caught speeding on the way home last week and received a ticket and $50 fine. ＿＿＿＿
14. My friend's professor singled him/her out as an excellent student and offered him/her a job in the department. ＿＿＿＿

EXERCISE 4

<u>EXAM RATING SCALE</u>

To what extent to you think your score on this test was due to:

1. This particular test--how easy or difficult it was:

    Not at all   0   1   2   3   4   5   6   7   8   9   To a great extent

2. My academic ability or lack of ability:

    Not at all   0   1   2   3   4   5   6   7   8   9   To a great extent

3. Study--how much or little I studied:

    Not at all   0   1   2   3   4   5   6   7   8   9   To a great extent

4. Luck--good or bad:

    Not at all   0   1   2   3   4   5   6   7   8   9   To a great extent

5. What score did you receive on the test?

    _____

6. How satisfied are you with this score?

    Not at all
     satisfied   0   1   2   3   4   5   6   7   8   9   Very satisfied

7. Was this test

    A poor measure   An excellent
     of what   measure of
      I knew   0   1   2   3   4   5   6   7   8   9   what I knew

8. Are you ___ female ___ male?

EXERCISE 6

APPLYING ATTRIBUTION TO EVERYDAY SITUATIONS

You need an expert mountain climber to come along on your next expedition, and you are trying to decide whether Scott is qualified for the job. One day you observe him climbing a difficult cliff. From another observer you learn that most climbers are unable to negotiate this particular cliff. You learn that Scott has climbed this cliff several other times without experiencing a mishap. You also learn that he has successfully climbed many cliffs of varying types.

1. In this example, consensus is high low (circle one)

2. Describe the consensus information:

3. In this example, consistency is high low (circle one)

4. Describe the consistency information:

5. In this example, distinctiveness is high low (circle one)

6. Describe the distinctiveness information:

7. Based on the information provided, should you take Scott on your mountain-climbing expedition? yes no (circle one)

    Why or why not?

EXERCISE 6 (Cont.)

You are trying to decide whether to go to a restaurant that has been recommended by a friend of yours. Ann says she has been there several times and liked it a lot each time no matter what kind of mood she was in. She also mentions that there aren't many restaurants that she likes. You have also heard from several other friends that this is a good restaurant.

1. In this example, consensus is high low (circle one)

2. Describe the consensus information:

3. In this example consistency is high low (circle one)

4. Describe the consistency information:

5. In this example distinctiveness is high low (circle one)

6. Describe the distinctiveness information:

7. Based on this information, should you go to this restaurant?
    yes no (circle one)

    Why or why not?

EXERCISE 3

INSTRUCTIONS: Read each of the following words, and indicate whether the word has an "e" in it by circling either "yes" or "no".

aggressive	yes	no
intelligent	yes	no
sociable	yes	no
superstitious	yes	no
quiet	yes	no
sentimental	yes	no
bold	yes	no
athletic	yes	no
persistent	yes	no
trusting	yes	no
sensitive	yes	no
energetic	yes	no
shy	yes	no

EXERCISE 3A

INSTRUCTIONS: Read each of the following words, and indicate whether the word describes you by circling either "yes" or "no".

aggressive	yes	no
intelligent	yes	no
sociable	yes	no
superstitious	yes	no
quiet	yes	no
sentimental	yes	no
bold	yes	no
athletic	yes	no
persistent	yes	no
trusting	yes	no
sensitive	yes	no
energetic	yes	no
shy	yes	no

EXERCISE 1

RATINGS OF TRUSTWORTHINESS OF OCCUPATIONS

Occupation	Most Trustworthy	Rating		Least Trustworthy
U.S. Army generals	1	2	3	4
College professor	1	2	3	4
Lawyers	1	2	3	4
TV repairmen	1	2	3	4
Psychologists	1	2	3	4
TV news reporters	1	2	3	4
Plumbers	1	2	3	4
Used car salesmen	1	2	3	4
Corporate executives	1	2	3	4
Clergy	1	2	3	4
Newspaper columnists	1	2	3	4
Physicians	1	2	3	4
Police officers	1	2	3	4
Dentists	1	2	3	4
Judges	1	2	3	4
Auto repairmen	1	2	3	4
High school teachers	1	2	3	4
Politicians	1	2	3	4
Labor union officials	1	2	3	4

EXERCISE 2

SELF-MONITORING SCALE

The statements that follow concern your personal reactions to a number of different situations. No two statements are exactly alike, so consider each statement carefully before answering. If a statement is TRUE or MOSTLY TRUE as applied to you, mark a "T" to the left of the statement. If a statement is FALSE or NOT USUALLY TRUE as applied to you, mark a "F" to the left of the statement. It is important that you answer as frankly and honestly as you can.

__ 1. I find it hard to imitate the behavior of other people.

__ 2. My behavior is usually an expression of my true inner feelings, attitudes and beliefs.

__ 3. At parties and social gatherings, I do not attempt to do or say things that others will like.

__ 4. I can only argue for ideas which I already believe.

__ 5. I can make impromptu speeches even on topics about which I have almost no information.

__ 6. I guess I put on a show to impress or entertain people.

__ 7. When I am uncertain how to act in a social situation, I look to the behavior of the others for cues.

__ 8. I would probably make a good actor.

__ 9. I rarely seek the advice of my friends to choose movies, books, or music.

__10. I sometimes appear to others to be experiencing deeper emotions than I actually am.

__11. I laugh more when I watch a comedy with others than when alone.

__12. In a group of people I am rarely the center of attention.

__13. In different situations and with different people, I often act like very different persons.

__14. I am not particularly good at making other people like me.

__15. Even if I am not enjoying myself, I often pretend to be having a good time.

__16. I'm not always the person I appear to be.

__17. I would not change my opinions (or the way I do things) in order to please someone else or win their favor.

EXERCISE 2 (Continued)

___ 18. I have considered being an entertainer.

___ 19. In order to get along and be liked, I tend to be what people expect me to be rather than anything else.

___ 20. I have never been good at games like charades or improvisational acting.

___ 21. I have trouble changing my behavior to suit different people and different situations.

___ 22. At a party I let others keep the jokes and stories going.

___ 23. If feel a bit awkward in company and do not show up quite so well as I should.

___ 24. I can look anyone in the eye and tell a lie with a straight face (if for a right end).

___ 25. I may deceive people by being friendly when I really dislike them.

EXERCISE 3

LOG SHEET

Date:_____ Sex:_____ Code Number:_____

Write down five words to describe yourself. Please, use only words, no phrases or sentences.

1. _____

2. _____

3. _____

4. _____

5. _____

Write down the most important thing that happened to you.

_____

_____

_____

_____

_____

EXERCISE 1

IS THERE RACISM AT THIS SCHOOL?

This is an anonymous survey written by students. Circle or mark all relevant responses--remember there is no ONE right answer. Any comments are encouraged. This is not a test. The survey will probably take about 15-20 minutes.

1. Here are some definitions of racism; check those that you agree with and leave blank those you disagree with.

____ Racism is when people aren't given or allowed equal opportunities because of their racial or ethnic background (For example Black, Asian, Jewish, White, Hispanic, Arab etc.)

____ Racism is whenever people are discriminated against.

____ Racism is when people are segregated according to which racial or ethnic background they are from.

____ Racism is when people hate, dislike or fear other people because of their racial or ethnic background.

____ Racism is something that degrades, demoralizes or hurts people because they are from a certain racial or ethnic group.

____ Other, please write your own definition _____

_____

EXERCISE 1

2. Is there racism at your school?   Yes / No / Other

    If yes

        a. In your school how is racism shown? (Check all that apply)?

        ___   Ethnic Slurs   ___   Threats against a person

        ___   Offensive remarks   ___   Threats against a group

        ___   Physical assault   ___   Exclusion

        ___   Physical intimidation   ___   Social segregation

        ___   Mocking stereotypes   ___   Other (be specific)

                                               _____

                                               _____

        b.   How do you know about racist incidents at your school? (Check all that apply)?

        ___   You've been in the incident

        ___   Someone told you of one

        ___   Rumors

        ___   You witnessed an incident

        ___   I know of no racist incidents at my school

        ___   Other _____

3. To what extent do you feel racism to be a serious problem in your school? (Rate on a scale of 1-5 with "1"=very serious, and "5"=not a problem at all.) Circle your choice 1 2 3 4 5

EXERCISE 1

4. What causes racism? (Check all that apply)

   ___   Feelings of inadequacy   ___   Peer pressure

   ___   Stereotypes   ___   Ignorance

   ___   Upbringing   ___   Fear

   ___   Past experiences   ___   Media

   ___   Other_____

5. Check the words or symbols you think are racist.

   ___   swastika   ___   "Jap" (Japanese)   ___   "chink"

   ___   "nigger"   ___   "JAP" (Jewish)   ___   "skinhead"

   ___   "white boy"

6. If you think some social groups are racially segregated, is it because (Check if you agree; leave blank those you disagree with.)

   ___   People come from different backgrounds

   ___   People stay with friends from their own neighborhoods

   ___   People have racist feelings

   ___   People from the same race or ethnic group have more in common

   ___   Other (please explain)_____

   ___   I don't think social groups are racially segregated

EXERCISE 1

7. Have you ever seen racism in any of these forms? (Check if yes, leave blank if no.)

    ___ Discrimination in textbooks

    ___ Faculty ignoring or singling out minority students

    ___ Faculty being more negative to minority students

    ___ Faculty presenting class material in a discriminatory way

    ___ Not enough minority faculty members

    ___ Other_____

8. Do you think that minority students discriminate against whites? (Circle one)

    Yes / No / I don't know

9. Do you and your friends discuss racism? Yes / No

10. Do you hold racist feelings? Yes / No / Other

    (explain "other")_____

The following questions are completely optional. The reason they are asked is not to be personal, but to find out if certain groups of people feel more or less strongly about racism. [82% answered these questions]

Sex: Male / Female

Year in school: 1st, 2nd, 3rd, 4th, 5th

What is your racial identity? (Ex. Black, Caucasian)_____

EXERCISE 2A

Imagine that you are encountering a person for the first time. Think of your subtle and overt

reactions to the stranger: your posture, amount of eye contact, tone of voice, content of what

you would say, willingness to talk, etc. Would the gender of the person make any difference in

your reactions? Indicate the degree to which gender would make a difference on the scale below.

---:---:---:---:---:---:---

sex of the   sex of the

person would   person would

make no diff-   make a great

erence   difference

EXERCISE 2B

Imagine that you are encountering a person for the first time. Think of your subtle and overt

reactions to the stranger: your posture, amount of eye contact, tone of voice, content of what

you would say, willingness to talk, etc. Would the race of the person make any difference in

your reactions? Indicate the degree to which race would make a difference on the scale below.

---:---:---:---:---:---:---

race of the   race of the

person would   person would

make no diff-   make a great

erence   difference

EXERCISE 4

DISCUSSION GROUP SEATING CHART

Position Two
name:

Position Three
name:

Position One:
leader's name:

Position Four:
name:

Position Five:
name:

EXERCISE 2

INTERPERSONAL ORIENTATION SCALE

If a particular statement describes your typical reaction or feelings about others very well, then it would be "Completely true" and you would write the letter "E." If a particular statement does <u>not</u> describe you well or is opposite of the way you feel, then it is "Not at all true" and you should write the letter "A." The scale to use in responding to each statement is as follows:

A	B	C	D	E
Not at all True	Slightly True	Somewhat True	Mostly True	Completely True

___ 1. One of my greatest sources of comfort when things get rough is being with other people.

___ 2. I prefer to participate in activities alongside other people rather than by myself because I like to see how I am doing on the activity.

___ 3. The main thing I like about being around other people is the warm glow I get from contact with them.

___ 4. It seems like whenever something bad or disturbing happens to me I often just want to be with a close, reliable friend.

___ 5. I mainly like people who seem strongly drawn to me and who seem infatuated with me.

___ 6. I think I get satisfaction out of contact with others more than most people realize.

___ 7. When I am not certain about how well I am doing at something, I usually like to be around others so I can compare myself to them.

___ 8. I like to be around people when I can be the center of attention.

___ 9. When I have not done very well on something that is very important to me, I can get to feeling better simply by being around other people.

___ 10. Just being around others and finding out about them is one of the most interesting things I can think of doing.

___ 11. I seem to get satisfaction from being with others more than a lot of other people do.

___ 12. If I am uncertain about what is expected of me, such as on a task or in a social situation, I usually like to be able to look to certain others for cues.

EXERCISE 2 (Continued)

___ 13. I feel like I have really accomplished something valuable when I am able to get close to someone.

___ 14. I find that I often have the desire to be around other people who are experiencing the same thing I am when I am unsure about what is going on.

___ 15. During times when I have to go through something painful. I usually find that having someone with me makes it less painful.

___ 16. I often have a strong need to be around people who are impressed with what I am like and what I do.

___ 17. If I feel unhappy or kind of depressed, I usually try to be around other people to make me feel better.

___ 18. I find that I often look to certain other people to see how I compare to others.

___ 19. I mainly like to be around others who think I am an important, exciting person.

___ 20. I think it would be satisfying if I could have very close friendships with quite a few people.

___ 21. I often have a very strong desire to get people I am around to notice me and appreciate what I am like.

___ 22. I don't like being with people who may give me less than positive feedback about myself.

___ 23. I usually have the greatest need to have other people around me when I feel upset about something.

___ 24. I think being close to others, listening to them, and relating to them on a one-to-one level is one of my favorite and most satisfying pastimes.

___ 25. I would find it very satisfying to be able to form new friendships with whomever I liked.

___ 26. One of the most enjoyable things I can think of that I like to do is just watching people and seeing what they are like.

EXERCISE 3

ROMANTICISM SCALE

Respond to the following 5 statements by indicating the degree to which you agree of disagree with the statement. Respond using the following scale for each statement:

		Neither		
Strongly Agree	Moderately Agree	Agree Nor Disagree	Moderately Disagree	Strongly Disagree
1	2	3	4	5

____1.   Economic security should be considered before selecting a marriage partner.

____2.   True love leads to almost perfect happiness.

____3.   Most of us could sincerely love any one of several people equally well.

____4.   If I were in love with someone, I would marry him/her regardless of his/her social class and family background.

____5.   A deep love for another can compensate for differences in religious and economic background.

EXERCISE 4

CHECKLIST

		SELF	FRIEND	NON-FRIEND
1.	active	_____	_____	_____
2.	aggressive	_____	_____	_____
3.	ambitious	_____	_____	_____
4.	belligerent	_____	_____	_____
5.	brave	_____	_____	_____
6.	dependent	_____	_____	_____
7.	dominant	_____	_____	_____
8.	gentle	_____	_____	_____
9.	helpful	_____	_____	_____
10.	independent	_____	_____	_____
11.	needs sympathy	_____	_____	_____
12.	obliging	_____	_____	_____
13.	passive	_____	_____	_____
14.	peaceful	_____	_____	_____
15.	protective	_____	_____	_____
16.	seeks protection	_____	_____	_____
17.	self-centered	_____	_____	_____
18.	self-confident	_____	_____	_____
19.	sociable	_____	_____	_____
20.	tactless	_____	_____	_____
21.	timid	_____	_____	_____
22.	unconventional	_____	_____	_____

EXERCISE 5

DATING SURVEY

1. Are you currently dating someone exclusively (that is, one person and no one else)? (Check one.)

   yes_____   no_____

2. If yes, how many months have you dated this person? _____

3. If you are not dating one person exclusively at the present time, have you dated at least two different people in the past year? (Check one.)

   yes_____   no_____

4. If yes, how many different persons have you dated in the past year? _____

5. If you are currently dating someone (whether exclusively or not), please write your current (or most steady) dating partner's initials on the first line below. Then write the initials of 3 opposite-sex friends on the lines that follow.

   Current partner_____

   Friend No. 1   _____

   Friend No. 2   _____

   Friend No. 3   _____

6. If you could ideally form a close, intimate dating relationship with either your current dating partner or Friend No. 1, whom would you choose?

7. If you could ideally form a close, intimate dating relationship with either your current dating partner or Friend No. 2, whom would you choose?

8. If you could ideally form a close, intimate dating relationship with either your current dating partner or Friend No. 3, whom would you choose?

EXERCISE 1a

IMAGINING THE LONELINESS OF EMOTIONAL ISOLATION

Read these instructions and then close your eyes and implement them

You live in an apartment. You are there alone. So far as your feelings go, you are entirely alone. You have no one to call, no one to talk to. There is no one sharing your life, no one at all. This is the way it is, this the way it is going to be. If you were to go out, you would still be alone.

Please take note in your mind of the way you feel.

After you have implemented the instructions, open your eyes and write down what your feelings are.

EXERCISE 1b

IMAGINING THE LONELINESS OF SOCIAL ISOLATION

Read the following instructions, then close your eyes and implement them

You are with someone with whom you are sharing your life, someone you are married to or are living with.

The two of you are in a part of country that is new and strange to you. You have been there for two months. You have seen all the movies and you have gone to several of the bars. People are pleasant but distant. The only people you have to talk to are each other. You don't really know anyone else in town. It is evening again and again it is just the two of you.

What are your feelings"? Please think of them now.

Write down your feelings as you thought of them.

Adapted from Weiss (1987).

EXERCISE 4

RATE YOUR FRIENDSHIP

Select one of your important friendships. By checking some point along each of the scales below each statement, indicate the degree to which each statement applies to your friendship.

Each of us accepts the other as he (she) is. We don't try to change each other.

--:--:--:--:--:--:--:--

clearly applies   clearly does not apply
to our relationship   to our relationship

We trust each other and feel we can count on each other.

--:--:--:--:--:--:--:--

clearly applies   clearly does not apply
to our relationship   to our relationship

We respect each other. We respect each other's advice, competence, and ability to "do the right thing."

--:--:--:--:--:--:--:--

clearly applies   clearly does not apply
to our relationship   to our relationship

We support each other. Each knows the other is "there for me."

--:--:--:--:--:--:--:--

clearly applies   clearly does not apply
to our relationship   to our relationship

We confide in each other. There is hardly anything we wouldn't tell one another.

--:--:--:--:--:--:--:--

clearly applies   clearly does not apply
to our relationship   to our relationship

We know what makes one another "tick." Each can decipher why the other is upset or troubled.

--:--:--:--:--:--:--:--

clearly applies   clearly does not apply
to our relationship   to our relationship

Spontaneity characterizes our relationship. We feel we can say or do whatever we want around one another.

--:--:--:--:--:--:--:--

clearly applies   clearly does not apply
to our relationship   to our relationship

EXERCISE 4 Continued

We are loyal to one another. We stand in each other's corner no matter what.

--:--:--:--:--:--:--:--:--

| clearly applies | clearly does not apply |
| to our relationship | to our relationship |

We are generous with each other. Each gives to the other and neither keeps scores.

--:--:--:--:--:--:--:--:--

| clearly applies | clearly does not apply |
| to our relationship | to our relationship |

We are honest with each other. We tell each other the truth, even if it hurts.

--:--:--:--:--:--:--:--:--

| clearly applies | clearly does not apply |
| to our relationship | to our relationship |

EXERCISE 1

SYMBOLS FOR THE STUDY OF AESTHETICS

	1	2	3	4	5
A.	Ω	≈	ç	√	∫
B.	~	µ	≤	≥	÷
C.	å	«	δ	ø	Θ
D.	η	Δ	ψ	…	æ
E.	Σ	´	Φ	†	¥
F.	§	˜	ˆ	ϕ	π
G.	β	‘	@	¦	™
H.	#	£	¢	∞	`
I.	¶	&	•	*	♭
J.	♮	+	!	≠	=

EXERCISE 3

ESTIMATES OF LEVEL OF OBEDIENCE

My Sex is ____ (M or F)   My age is__

How many U. S. citizens out of 100 would obey fully and use all the switches including the one marked "450 volts?" [circle one number]

     10 15 20 25 30 35 40 45 50 55 60 65 70 75 80 85 90 95 100

I myself would ____ would not ____ obey fully and use all the switches including the one marked "450 volts?" [check "would" or "would not"]

____   "Before today, I had never before heard of the Milgram obedience experiment or I have heard about it but can't remember anything significant about it?"

____   "I have heard about the Milgram obedience experiment and have at least some recollection regarding its results.

EXERCISE 1

IS IT PROSOCIAL BEHAVIOR?

<u>Yes</u>   <u>No</u>

1. John, a college student, spends two hours per week as a "Big Brother" to a nine-year-old boy whose parents are divorced.   ____ ____

   Why or why not?

2. Arnold, a firefighter, rescues an elderly woman trapped in a fire.   ____ ____

   Why or why not?

3. Sandra agrees to donate her organs for transplant in the event of her death.   ____ ____

   Why or why not?

4. Marie makes a $50 contribution to charity and thus gets a chance to attend a banquet with a celebrity.   ____ ____

   Why or why not?

5. Bob attempts to save his six-year-old son from drowning.   ____ ____

   Why or why not?

6. Tom informs the manager of the bookstore about a college student who shoplifted a book.   ____ ____

   Why or why not?

7. Ann makes an anonymous donation of $1,000 to her church's building fund.   ____ ____

   Why or why not?

8. Marty buys a raffle ticket from a charitable organization.   ____ ____

   Why or why not?

EXERCISE 2

Indicate the number of times in the past month that you have performed each of the following actions.

_____ 1. I have assisted someone experiencing car trouble (changing a tire, calling a mechanic, pushing a stalled or stuck car, etc.).

_____ 2. I have given someone directions.

_____ 3. I have made change for someone.

_____ 4. I have given money to charity.

_____ 5. I have given money to someone who needed it (or asked for it).

_____ 6. I have done volunteer work for charity.

_____ 7. I have donated blood.

_____ 8. I have helped carry another person's belongings (books, parcels, etc.)

_____ 9. I have delayed an elevator and held the door open for another.

_____ 10. I have allowed someone to go ahead of me in a line (in the supermarket, during registration, etc.).

_____ 11. I have another a ride in my car.

_____ 12. I have pointed out a clerk's error (in a bank, at the supermarket, etc.) in undercharging me for an item.

_____ 13. I have let someone borrow an item of some value to me (clothes, jewelry, stereo, etc.).

_____ 14. I have helped another with a homework assignment when my knowledge was greater than his or hers.

_____ 15. I have voluntarily looked after another's plants, pets, house, or children without being paid for it.

_____ 16. I have offered my seat in a crowed room or on a train or bus to someone who was standing

_____ 17. I have helped another to move his or her possessions to another room, apartment, or house.

EXERCISE 2 (Continued)

___ 18. I have retrieved an item dropped by another for him or her (pencil, book, packages, etc.)

___ 19. I have held the door open to a room or building for another to enter.

___ 20. I have helped another with a personal project (painting, repairing a car, etc.)

___ 21 I have helped one or more people in an emergency involving the threat or sustenance of bodily injury to the victim(s).

EXERCISE 1

COMMUNICATOR EVALUATION FORM

On the scale below each statement check a point between the words "agree" and "disagree" to indicate the extent to which you agree or disagree with the statement. Use any point you wish.

The communicator was convincing.

agree_1_:_2_:_3_:_4_:_5_:_6_:_7_disagree

The communicator was expert about the topic covered.

agree_1_:_2_:_3_:_4_:_5_:_6_:_7_disagree

The communicator is a trustworthy source of information.

agree_1_:_2_:_3_:_4_:_5_:_6_:_7_disagree

The communicator is a likable person.

agree_1_:_2_:_3_:_4_:_5_:_6_:_7_disagree

I tend to think like the communicator.

agree_1_:_2_:_3_:_4_:_5_:_6_:_7_disagree

The communicator is a generally knowledgeable person.

agree_1_:_2_:_3_:_4_:_5_:_6_:_7_disagree

I would like to learn what the communicator knows about

other topics.

agree_1_:_2_:_3_:_4_:_5_:_6_:_7_disagree

EXERCISE 2

UNDERSTANDING AGGRESSION FORM INSTRUCTIONS

First, fix in mind an aggressive act committed by someone. It can be real or imaginary. Below are three categories of reasons why the person has committed the aggressive act. List reasons for the act that fall into the three categories. First, list reasons that relate to the target of the attack. For example, the target insulted the aggressor. Second, list reasons related to people other than the target of the attack. For example, the aggressor just was humiliated by his or her brother, and the target happened to be handy when the aggression exploded. Third, list reasons related to the aggressor's feelings about him or herself or his or her skills and efforts. For example, the aggressor may feel bad about herself or himself, because his or her application for a desirable job has just been turned down.

Reasons for aggression relating to target of aggression

[List reasons for the aggressive act that relate to the target of the aggression]
I think that the student believes the professor has been made an unfair test.
Possibly the student just doesn't like the professor...personalities sometimes clash.
The professor was unsympathetic when the student came up to complain about the test.

Reasons for aggression relating to persons other than
the target

It looked to me that the student was in a bad mood. Probably his girlfriend jilted him or something like that.
My guess is that this guy has just been pushed around too much. Maybe he came to class with a chip on his shoulder, because his friends have been teasing him.
One possibility is that he has trouble at work. Maybe the boss has been on his back.

Reasons relating to the aggressor's feelings about
self or abilities and efforts

This guy looked like he was down on himself. I think he has low self-esteem.
It seems possible to me that this individual has been used to failing. He has lost confidence that he can succeed in school.
This student...he is socially inept. He just doesn't know how to register a complaint.

EXERCISE 3

AGGRESSION QUESTIONNAIRE

1. A spider eats a fly.
2. Two wolves fight for the leadership of the pack.
3. A soldier shoots an enemy at the front line.
4. The warden of a prison executes a convicted criminal.
5. A juvenile gang attacks members of another gang.
6. Two men fight for a piece of bread.
7. A man viciously kicks a cat.
8. A man, while cleaning a window, knocks over a flowerpot, which, in falling, injures a pedestrian.
9. A girl kicks a wastebasket.
10. Mr. X, a notorious gossip, speaks disparagingly of many people of his acquaintance.
11. A men mentally rehearses a murder he is about to commit.
12. An angry son purposely fails to write to his mother, who is expecting a letter and will be hurt if none arrives.
13. An enraged boy tries with all his might to inflict injury on his antagonist, a bigger boy, but is not successful in doing so. His efforts simply amuse the bigger boy.
14. A man daydreams of harming his antagonist, but has no hope of doing so.
15. A senator does not protest the escalation of bombing to which he is morally opposed.
16. A farmer beheads a chicken and prepares if for supper.
17. A hunter kills an animal and mounts it as a trophy.
18. A dog snarls at a mail carrier, but does not bite.
19. A physician give a flu shot to a screaming child.
20. A boxer give his opponent a bloody nose.
21. A Girl Scout tries to assist an elderly women, but trips her by accident.
22. A bank robber is shot in the back while trying to escape.
23. A tennis player smashes his racket after missing a volley.
24. A person commits suicide.
25. A cat kills a mouse, parades around with it, and the discards it.

EXERCISE 4a

HOSTILITY QUESTIONNARIE

1. When anybody slows down or stops what I want to do, I think they are selfish, mean and inconsiderate.

    Never   Sometimes   Often   Always

2. When anybody does something that seems incompetent, messy, selfish, or inconsiderate to me, I quickly feel angry or enraged. At the same time, my heart races, my breath comes quickly and my palms sweat.

    Never   Sometimes   Often   Always

3. When I have such thoughts or feelings (No. 2), I let fly with words, gestures, a raised voice and frowns.

    Never   Sometimes   Often   Always

EXERCISE 4b

TWELVE STEPS TO A MORE TRUSTING HEART

1. Monitor your cynical thoughts by recognizing them.

2. Confess your hostility and seek support for change.

3. Stop cynical thoughts.

4. Reason with yourself.

5. Put yourself in the other guy's shoes.

6. Laugh at yourself.

7. Practice relaxing.

8. Try trusting others.

9. Force yourself to listen more.

10. Substitute assertiveness (firmness) for aggression.

11. Pretend today is your last day.

12. Practice forgiveness.

EXERCISE 1

IS IT A GROUP?

For each of the following, indicate whether the situation describes a group. Indicate the reason(s) for your decision in the space beneath each example.

<u>Is This a Group?</u>

	<u>yes</u>	<u>no</u>
1. The people riding together on an airliner	____	____
2. The 22,000 people attending a rock concert	____	____
3. The students taking this course	____	____
4. The members of a particular labor union	____	____
5. People riding together on an elevator	____	____
6. The members of a particular fraternity on campus	____	____
7. The employees of General Motors	____	____
8. The members of the school debating team	____	____
9. The employees of your school's Financial Aid Office	____	____
10. The "starting five" on a basketball team	____	____
11. All the students enrolled at your university	____	____

EXERCISE 2

CHOICE DILEMMAS QUESTIONNAIRE

Alan, an electrical engineer, who is married and has one child, has been working for a large electronics corporation since graduating from college five years ago. He is assured of a lifetime job with a modest, though adequate, salary, and liberal pension benefits upon retirement. On the other hand, it is very unlikely that his salary will increase much before he retires. While attending a convention, Alan is offered a job with a small, newly founded company which has a highly uncertain future. The new job would pay more to start and would offer the possibility of a share in the ownership if the company survived the competition of the larger firms.

Imagine that you are advising Alan. What is the <u>lowest</u> probability or odds of the new company's proving financially sound that you would consider acceptable for Alan to take the new job?

The chances should be _____ in 10 that the company will prove financially sound.

Betty, a newlywed, has been informed by her physician that a heart ailment makes it inadvisable for her to have children. Having been an only child, Betty had always hoped to raise a large family herself. The physician suggests that a delicate medical operation could be attempted which, if successful, would completely relieve the heart condition. But its success could not be assured, and, in fact, the operation might prove fatal.

Imagine that you are advising Betty. What is the <u>lowest</u> probability or odds that the operation will prove successful that you would consider acceptable for the operation to be performed?

The chances should be _____ in 10 that the operation will be a success.

Peter is an earnest young state representative who would like to run for governor of his state. Since he has a reputation as an able and conscientious legislator, several influential persons have pledged their support to him should he decide to run. But his opponent would be the incumbent governor who has a well-organized political machine behind him, so it would not be an easy campaign.

Imagine that you are advising Peter. What is the <u>lowest</u> probability or odds of Peter's winning the election that would make it worthwhile for Peter to run for this office?

The chances should be _____ in 10 that Peter would win the election.

Henry is a writer who is said to have considerable creative talent but who so far has been earning a comfortable living by writing cheap Westerns.
Recently, he has come up with an idea for a potentially significant novel. If it would be written and accepted, it might have considerable literary impact and be a big boost to his career. On the other hand, if he was not able to work out his idea or if the novel was a flop, he would have expended considerable time and energy without remuneration.

Imagine that you are advising Henry. What is the <u>lowest</u> probability or odds of the novel's being a success that you would consider acceptable for Henry to attempt to write the novel?

The chances should be _____ in 10 that the novel will be a success.

EXERCISE 2 (Continued)

Mark is contemplating marriage to Susan, a girl whom he has known for a little more than a year. Recently, however, a number of arguments have occurred between them, suggesting some sharp differences of opinion in the way each views certain matters. Indeed, they decided to seek professional advice from a marriage counselor as to whether it would be wise for them to marry. On the basis of these meetings with a marriage counselor, they realize that a happy marriage, while possible, would not be assured.

Imagine that you are advising Mark and Susan. What is the <u>lowest</u> probability or odds that their marriage would prove to be a happy and successful one that you would consider acceptable for Mark and Susan to get married.

The chances should be _____ in 10 that the marriage would be happy and successful.

George, a competent chess player, is participating in a national chess tournament. In an early match he draws the top-favored player in the tournament as his opponent. George has been given a relatively low ranking in view of his performance in previous tournaments. During the course of his play with the top-favored man, George notes the possibility of a deceptive, though risky, maneuver which might bring him a quick victory. At the same time, if the attempted maneuver should fail, George would be left in an exposed position and defeat would almost certainly follow.

Imagine that you are advising George. What is the <u>lowest</u> probability or odds that the deceptive play would succeed that you would consider acceptable for George to attempt the play?

The chances should be _____ in 10 that the play would succeed.

EXERCISE 4

SKILLS NEEDED IN TODAY'S LEADERS

For each of the following skills or traits, indicate the degree to which you think the characteristic is important for a political leader in today's world. Use the following scale in making your ratings: 1 = extremely important; 2 = very important; 3 = important; 4 = somewhat important; 5 = not important.

Political ability	1	2	3	4	5
Common sense	1	2	3	4	5
Intellectual excellence	1	2	3	4	5
Courage	1	2	3	4	5
Social concern	1	2	3	4	5
Moral integrity	1	2	3	4	5
Charisma	1	2	3	4	5
Grasp of economics	1	2	3	4	5
Foreign-affairs expertise	1	2	3	4	5

EXERCISE 2

VALUE SCALE

Rank

A comfortable life

An exciting life

A sense of accomplishment

A world at peace

A world of beauty

A clean environment in the future

Family security

Free use of the environment now

Happiness

Inner harmony

Mature love

National security

Pleasure

Salvation

Self-respect

Social recognition

True friendship

Wisdom

EXERCISE 3

NUMBER OF CASES OF VARIOUS DISEASE ACCUMULATED
DURING THE FIRST 19 WEEKS OF 1990

Measles

Rabies (humans)

Gonorrhea

AIDS

Botulism (contamination of food)

Tetanus

Syphilis   17,539

Tuberculosis

Leprosy

Typhoid fever

Exercise 4: The Social Readjustment Scale

Events	Score	Rank	Events	Score	Rank
Death of a spouse			Change in responsibilities at work		
Divorce			Son or daughter leaving home		
Marital separation			Trouble with in-laws		
Jail term			Outstanding personal achievement		
Death of close family member			Spouse begins or stops work ("wife" originally)		
Personal injury or illness			Begin or end school		
Marriage			Change in living conditions		
Fired at work			Revision of personal habits		
Marital reconciliation			Trouble with boss		
Retirement			Change in work hours or conditions		
Change in health of family member			Change in residence		
Pregnancy			Change in schools		
Sex difficulties			Change in recreation		
Gain of new family member			Change in church activities		
Business readjustment			Change in social activities		
Change in financial state			Small mortgage or loan		
Death of close friend			Change in sleeping habits		
Change to different line of work			Change in number of family get-to-gethers		
Change in no. of arguments with spouse			Change in eating habits		
High mortgage			Vacation Christmas		
Foreclosure of mortgage or loan			Minor violation of Law		

EXERCISE 5

ACTUAL U. S. FATALITIES AND RANKS FOR SEVERAL DISEASES AND FOR ACCIDENTS

DISEASE (OR ACCIDENTS)	FATALITIES	RANK
smallpox		
tuberculosis		
accidents	93,990	
stroke		
diabetes		
cancer		
infectious hepatitis		
heart disease		
syphilis		
chronic lung disease		
measles		

Chapter Fourteen

EXERCISE 3

STUDENT GOVERNMENT PRESIDENTIAL ELECTION BALLOT

CANDIDATE	VOTE
Sarah Smithers	___
Ralph McLeRoy	___
Josh Monroe	___
Karen Foster	___
Suzanne Albert	___
Preston Sims	___
Anne Harvey	___
Kate Sampson	___
Shane Jackson	___
Marvin Allen	___
Rudy Anderson	___
Jennie Harper	___

EXERCISE 4

FIRST BALLOT

FIRST NAME OF JUROR   "GUILTY" OR "NOT GUILTY" VOTE

SECOND BALLOT

FIRST NAME OF JUROR   "GUILTY" OR "NOT GUILTY" VOTE

THIRD BALLOT

FIRST NAME OF JUROR   "GUILTY" OR "NOT GUILTY" VOTE

FOURTH BALLOT

FIRST NAME OF JUROR   "GUILTY" OR "NOT GUILTY" VOTE

FIFTH BALLOT

FIRST NAME OF JUROR   "GUILTY" OR "NOT GUILTY" VOTE

SIXTH BALLOT

FIRST NAME OF JUROR   "GUILTY" OR "NOT GUILTY" VOTE